SAME BED,
DIFFERENT DREAMS

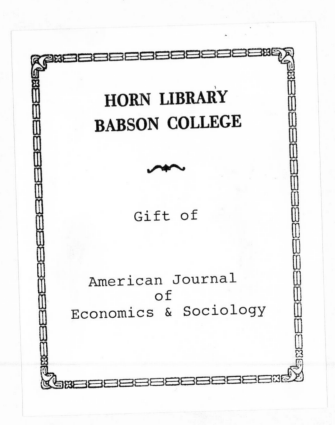

SAME BED, DIFFERENT DREAMS

America and Japan—Societies in Transition

EDITED BY
ALAN D. ROMBERG
TADASHI YAMAMOTO

COUNCIL ON FOREIGN RELATIONS PRESS
NEW YORK • LONDON

COUNCIL ON FOREIGN RELATIONS BOOKS

For more information about Council publications, please write the Council on Foreign Relations, 58 East 68th Street, New York, NY 10021, or call the Publications Office at (212) 734-0400.

Library of Congress Cataloguing-in-Publication Data

Same bed, different dreams : America and Japan—societies in transition
    / edited by Alan D. Romberg and Tadashi Yamamoto.
      p. cm.
    ISBN 0-87609-082-X
      1. United States—Relations—Japan. 2. Japan—Relations—United
States. 3. Industrial sociology—United States. 4. Industrial
sociology—Japan. 5. United States—Social conditions—1980–
6. Japan—Social conditions—1945– I. Romberg, Alan D.
II. Yamamoto, Tadashi.
E183.8.J3S215 1990
303.48'273052–dc20   90–1523
                                                                              CIP

96   95   94   93   92   91   90   PB   10   9   8   7   6   5   4   3   2   1

CONTENTS

LIST OF FIGURES AND TABLES

FIGURES

TABLES

PREFACE

Former Speaker of the House of Representatives **Tip O'Neill** used to say that all politics is local. By this he meant that in the end, people are concerned principally with how they and their community are affected by any given issue, however broadly that issue may be framed. In the same sense, all international politics is national. That is, foreign policy and international relations reflect domestic interests and values. Not everyone, of course, will interpret those interests and values in the same way, or draw the same policy conclusions from them. Nonetheless, to understand a nation's foreign policy, one must understand the domestic scene.

The current concern in both the United States and Japan about the nature and course of their future relations tends to focus on the headline issues of the day—typically, controversy over trade in semiconductors and supercomputers, or the need for better cooperation in defense, or uncertainty over how the two nations might conduct themselves with respect to Third World debt or foreign aid. The debate—and that is what it is becoming in both countries—takes place in a framework of the paradoxical twin realities of rapidly growing economic, political, and security interdependence, on the one hand, and commercial—and, increasingly, national—competition, on the other.

The depth of the interdependence is truly astounding, to an extent that is not fully comprehended in either country. In recent years, the critics and bashers have tended to dominate the debate in the United States until something has happened to pinch the vast "silent majority" that benefits from the relationship. Then, as we saw when the Congress sought to restrict broad categories of Toshiba products from entering the United States after a Toshiba subsidiary illegally sold sensitive equipment to the Soviet Union, Americans have spoken up. The Toshiba matter was serious and no one wanted to let it go unresponded to, but neither did anyone want it to be at his expense. In Japan, the sharpness and occasional anger of the rhetoric are only beginning to approach American levels, but they are rising, and those who value the relationship are now having to exert more effort.

Both the substance of the trade disputes, which involves commercial as well as government interests on both sides, and the increasingly acerbic style employed in negotiations and public debate threaten not only to cause temporary dislocations in U.S.-Japan relations, but over time to have an eroding effect that is much more serious and much more permanent.

The 28 people from both sides of the Pacific who gathered at Oiso, Japan, on December 10–11, 1988 (listed in the appendix), to discuss social and attitudinal changes in the United States and Japan and their implications for bilateral relations made no effort to hide their strong conviction about the importance of sustaining and strengthening the relationship, or their concern about some of the current trends. Their approach, however, was not to argue the merits of opening markets or being "fair." Building on an earlier effort in San Francisco* they set out to look behind the policies, practices, and problems of the moment to try to understand some of the more basic aspects of both societies and how they are changing.

The heart of this volume is the six chapters written by experts in the United States and Japan on evolving social attitudes and values in their own society, on what we loosely called industrial culture, and on the changing roles of politicians and bureaucrats in each country in setting the agenda and making policy. The lead-in chapter draws upon those papers and, even more important, upon the two days of intensive discussion at Oiso to come to some tentative conclusions about the implications of these domestic factors for the bilateral relationship.

None of this pretends to be definitive. Still, the sponsors and participants in the conference felt that it was important not only to identify key factors, but also to engage thoughtful Japanese and Americans from various sectors of society in dialogue about

---

* See Alan D. Romberg, *The United States and Japan: Changing Societies in a Changing Relationship,* A Conference Report (New York: Council on Foreign Relations, 1987).

them. The harsh reality of the persistent $50 billion or more trade imbalance, as well as complaints about specific problems, will create tensions regardless of the level of understanding. However, without some deeper appreciation of what drives each society, it will be far more difficult to cope with the strains that do exist—strains that, if ignored or mismanaged, threaten to disrupt a partnership essential for both.

The authors of these essays and all of the other participants gave enormously of themselves in a wide-ranging and penetrating discussion at Oiso. Their views are not generally attributed by name in chapter 1, and of course they are not responsible for the way those views were incorporated or adapted. But that essay is in important measure a product of what the author gleaned from their contributions.

Special appreciation is due to Tadashi Yamamoto, President of the Japan Center for International Exchange (JCIE), coeditor of this book, and to Professor Sadako Ogata, Vice President of the National Institute for Research Advancement (NIRA) and Dean of Faculty of Foreign Studies at Sophia University. Mr. Yamamoto and Professor Ogata, along with their colleagues at JCIE and NIRA—the two organizations that cosponsored the Oiso conference with the Council on Foreign Relations—devoted substantial time and energy to conceptualizing and organizing the conference and to enlisting the help of the outstanding scholars whose essays appear in this volume.

Joining the Council and NIRA in funding the conference were the Alfred P. Sloan Foundation of New York and the Foundation for Advanced Information and Research of Tokyo. Without their vision, commitment, and generosity, none of this would have been possible.

Alan D. Romberg
C. V. Starr Fellow for Asia
Council on Foreign Relations

New York
March 1990

1

THE UNITED STATES AND JAPAN: GRAPPLING WITH THE FUTURE

Alan D. Romberg

The United States and Japan are both grappling with changing realities to define their national identity and national purpose. In the recent past, Japanese have tended to see their country as a small and homogeneous nation, dedicated principally to its own economic well-being, but vulnerable to larger, international forces over which it has had little or no control. Since 1945, Japanese have not only shunned a significant military role, but have shied away from any high-profile international political activity, as well. Americans, on the other hand, have tended to see their society as a dynamic and open one on the rise, a leader that has stood for promotion of social justice and freedom not only at home but, especially since World War II, abroad, as well. Although they continue to struggle with the legacy of racial discrimination, Americans have valued their history as a "nation of immigrants," seeing it as giving them great strength and providing a living example of tolerance and openness for the world. Whether accurate or not, these have been the governing perceptions of the majority in each country.

But these self-images are slowly—and painfully—being eroded as the Japanese begin to internalize the reality of their great economic power and as Americans increasingly question their own strength and leadership position.

For a variety of reasons—in the early postwar years, largely because of a shared anticommunist perspective; later on, increasingly as a consequence of phenomenal growth in economic, political, and security links—these two very different societies have moved from a quite clear situation of inequality and dependence to a rather less well-defined one of interdependence, partnership, and shared global responsibility. Even in the best of

1

times, the tensions caused by such a change—both within each society and in the relationship between them—would have required enormous skill to manage. When, as in the past ten years, a shift in economic power has generated exceptionally competitive attitudes and resentments, and when each has felt the other was not living up to its responsibilities, the challenge has become all the greater, and the development of solutions all the more difficult.

The "answers" do not lie only in greater understanding. Indeed, more clarity in each country about the nature of the other society may actually exacerbate the problem in some measure, with people self-righteously asking: Why can't you be more like us? Still, without a broad comprehension—in government and the private sector—of the basic attitudes and values that drive each other and of the political, social, and economic dynamics that shape policies, we have little hope of avoiding an eventual weakening, and perhaps rending, of the relationship.

Some would argue that, however good one's intentions, the pace and scope of change are so great that they are unmanageable. Perhaps. But a starting point of this analysis is that even where governments and bodies politic cannot find specific solutions, with clearer understanding of the problem, they can at least shape the political, legal, and regulatory environment to help move things in a desirable direction. Without trying to draw in all of the points made in the succeeding chapters, what is attempted here is an assessment of some of the basic domestic factors in both countries—as well as the disconnects between them—and their implications for the relationship in the years to come.

AN ERA OF CHANGE

For all of the growing fears and defensiveness of many Americans, and all of the rising confidence and assertiveness (in some cases, arrogance) of many Japanese, the fact is that the United States remains the strongest economic and military power in the world and that it retains—and others, including Japan, wish it to retain—its political leadership role, as well. And despite the sense of "threat" from Japan that recent American polls purport to show, Japan does not, and on the whole does not want to, pose a challenge to this American preeminence.

What has changed, however, is the *relative* economic power of each country and, with it, the sense that each society has about its current and future standing. Japanese are increasingly under pressure to live up to the responsibilities that others believe their extraordinary development imposes on them; Americans are under pressure to share not just burdens but also power to a degree that they have not had to do since the end of World War II. Both peoples are uncertain about the implications for themselves and are uncomfortable with the potential adjustments.

Much that is "different" in each society, of course, is enduring, and, as will be alluded to at various points below, the notion of convergence between them is often exaggerated. Still, changes in attitudes and values are under way in both countries that in some cases could facilitate the adjustments, in others work against them.

Japan

Several developments within Japan could contribute to a healthier bilateral relationship. With the level of affluence in Japan now high and still rising, Sumiko Iwao (in chapter 3) sees decreasing emphasis on material reward for work and more on the quality of life, acceleration of movement toward diversity and individualism, greater concern for consumers' interests, and more openness to foreign ideas and values. These trends would seem to push in the direction of less intense competitiveness, more rapid opening of Japan's markets to imports, and keener sensitivity to such significant issues as minority hiring by overseas subsidiaries.

Positive ties are also facilitated by the fact that Japanese affinity for the United States has remained rather steady, despite some recent questioning of American reliability and growing resentment at perceived U.S. high-handedness in trade negotiations. Moreover, although the initiative came from the sense of international crisis (due largely to American pressure), the basic changes toward openness in Japan's economic structure and policy called for in the so-called Maekawa Report of 1986 have been broadly supported in that country.

And while change has been very slow in coming, there are signs that as Japanese corporations gain experience overseas, they *are* changing their attitudes and behavior in accommodating ways (see Haruo Shimada's analysis in chapter 5). This is true not only with respect to employment practices of many Japanese firms abroad, but also in the area of capital formation, where international sourcing is, at least to a limited extent, replacing the various domestic interlocking banking and business relationships that have up to now been seen as giving the Japanese a decided advantage.

At the same time, however, other trends in Japan are less encouraging, including the persistence of certain deeply ingrained attitudes and patterns of behavior that could limit the potential for change. Professor Iwao, for example, points to growing demand for instant gratification, especially among young people. This could tend to reduce savings—a key factor in Japan's competitive edge—thus easing the trade problems. But with its underlying requirement to preserve and enhance spending power, it could also reinforce the drive to compete successfully.

Iwao also notes the higher levels of national confidence— even feelings of superiority—and the emphasis Japanese place on protecting the good life that they have attained. While these attitudes are not necessarily inconsistent with greater openness, the importance attached to self-preservation and the sense that they are "doing it right" could mean less flexibility in inviting competition, or yielding in negotiations, rather than more.

Beyond that, other observers question how far diversity and individuality really go in Japan, seeing only a limited degree of change within what one Japanese at Oiso called a "wider straitjacket" of unity and homogeneity.

The growing role of Japanese women in positions of responsibility lags behind developments in the United States, but it is significant nonetheless. Still, the question arises whether this is transforming the workplace into a more "humane" environment, as Professor Iwao judges, or whether the women are doing the adapting. If the former is the case, then the confrontational nature of Japanese competitiveness may abate over time; if the latter, then the effect could be to sharpen bilateral tensions (which, as suggested below, may be taking place in America).

Moreover, while Japanese corporate behavior may be becoming "globalized" in some respects, it clearly is not in others. Japanese corporate culture tends to be very inward-looking and to focus on efficiency and competitiveness to the virtual exclusion of other considerations (for example, social justice, corporate citizenship, and conflicting demands on the time of employees and their families). It gives great weight to what it perceives (not entirely correctly) to be Japan's homogeneous society. These attitudes fit well into the Japanese scene, where the government has fostered fierce oligopolistic competition and has been responsible for dealing with the "weaker" elements of society that cannot keep up, as well as with any "public interest" issues. But they do not fit into the model of corporate behavior in the United States, and, as Japanese foreign direct investment has grown, so have tensions.

In the postwar years, when Japan was struggling back to its feet, bureaucratic experts played a particularly important role in developing and implementing policy. Although the international pressures on Japan at that time were not nearly so great as now, when there was a requirement to act on the international scene, the government was essentially able to do so without great concern for domestic opinion. In part, this was because the bureaucracy reflected cultural values reasonably well; in part, it was because public opinion had little opportunity to express itself on specific issues. (The 1960 revision of the U.S.–Japan Mutual Security Treaty was a prominent and troublesome exception.) Among other things, this facilitated the government's taking a long-term perspective rather than always having to look at the short-term payoff.

As Taizo Yakushiji points out (in chapter 7), however, although even today the central political system is still structured for the reconstruction era, once the recovery was completed, the relative strength of locally based, constituent-oriented, less-visionary politicians began to grow. Despite the continuing strength of producer (as opposed to consumer) interests, and despite the overall mistrust of politicians in Japan, especially on the part of increasingly active female voters, the attack on the Liberal Democratic Party's monopoly on power in 1989 seems to have been at least as much a reflection of voter concerns about specific government policies (for instance, the consumption tax and the total liberalization of the beef and citrus markets) as it was a reaction to the accompanying political scandals.

Despite these constraints, the growing sense of national pride, the realization that for Japan to get along in the world it must assume more responsibilities both to open up its society to international influences and to take risks as a world leader, and the pressures generated by the new images flooding Japan as a result of the communications and information revolution—all of these create a receptive mood among wider and wider circles of Japanese to new ways of thinking and behaving that will not necessarily lead to a convergence with the rest of the industrialized world, but that at least will facilitate accommodation with it.

The United States

Conflicting factors are also present in the United States. Working in the direction of smoother relations with Japan, polls show a greater openness—toward women, blacks, religious minorities, and foreigners (see Howard Schuman's discussion in chapter 2). Moreover, as Bert Rockman explains (in chapter 6), the presidential role has been strengthened, suggesting that if the President wants to achieve something, he usually does not feel very constrained by bureaucratic and other interests from going after it. (Whether he is ultimately frustrated by Congress, the bureaucracy, or other interests is another matter.)

American attitudes toward Japan remain generally positive, mirroring the constant Japanese affinity for the United States discussed above. Just as Japanese see lessons for themselves in the free-spirited American educational system, Americans see Japan's attention to academic excellence in primary and secondary school as something worth emulating, if perhaps in less single-minded ways. Despite the sharp sense of commercial competition, this admiration for Japanese performance is also seen in American corporate behavior, where attempts to adopt (or at least adapt) certain Japanese management techniques are notable. Although cultural differences limit the effectiveness of such "borrowing," many business executives see the spur of Japanese competition as having shaken American industry out of its lethargy and put it on a much more competitive footing. The extent of cross-border joint ventures is growing daily, enmeshing the interests of American and Japanese business in ways that are increasingly inextricable. The volume of transnational capital flows locks the two societies together to a degree that dwarfs the significance of trade imbalances.

Perhaps the most positive aspect in the United States is the recognition by the most senior government and business leaders of the enormous benefits of a cooperative relationship with Japan and the unthinkable costs of a hostile one. Even when they flirt with such delicate issues as amending the agreement on the cooperative development and production of the next-generation Japanese fighter aircraft (the so-called FSX), in the end they have come up with sensible decisions.

Arrayed against these positive factors are a host of negative pressures. Most basically, despite the continuing underlying strength of the United States, Americans seem ill at ease regarding their future. At times of confidence and economic certainty, the American system tolerates differences rather well. Affluence and a sense of fundamental security have given Americans the luxury of great choice, of emphasizing nonmaterial aspects of life—"being rather than having," as one of our conference participants put it.

But American-style heterogeneity does not work as well in times of adversity, when opportunities are shrinking. Especially in the international climate of renewed East-West détente, the sense of "threat" to the economic well-being of Americans that polls are now picking up could overwhelm the tendency toward openness, not only offsetting the improvement in attitudes toward domestic minorities but also leading to scapegoating of the perceived most important foreign source of many of America's problems—Japan.

Experts see this danger especially in the growing stratification of American society, with perhaps half of the population participating in the overall growth in national wealth, but with the other half deprived of the college education increasingly necessary to secure well-paying jobs and, thus, to share in the benefits of the "good life." This problem affects not only minorities but the whole society, and, as the perception of "winners" and "losers" grows, frustrations are likely to be taken out on those "responsible" for the situation.

Whether justified in their judgments or not, to the extent that Americans see themselves striving for social justice and equity while the Japanese are seen to concentrate on competition and economic efficiency, the problem will grow. We see signs of this even today, especially in the case of Japanese investment in the United States. If current trends continue, the resentments created by these perceptions will be exacerbated.

The American system of government does not lend itself particularly well to broad-gauged thinking and long-term planning, and this, too, has implications for U.S.–Japan relations. Beyond the strengthening of the presidential role, one of the other things that Professor Rockman shows us is that the competition between presidential and congressional staffs has led to a diminished role for the professional civil service. Compounded by the intensified partisanship that has resulted from recent Democratic dominance of the Congress and Republican dominance of the White House, and by budget constraints that limit the opportunity for innovative program development, this competition has led to a vacuum in policy formulation. As one observer who has played the game intensely from both the executive and the legislative side has put it:

> Since the late '60s traditional inter-branch rivalry has become a nasty, sometimes vicious brawl. Nowadays, it isn't enough to defeat an administration's policy goals . . . political opponents are viewed as enemies. . . . This fierce, even vicious partisanship makes cooperation in the conduct of the public's business difficult, and sometimes impossible. While either branch can act without the other on domestic and even most foreign policy matters, both have endless opportunities for sniping, blocking, recriminating and other sports. . . . The system of checks and balances has been replaced by a system of checks and cross-checks. . . . It is just so damn hard to get anything done.[1]

Beyond these institutional factors within government, the U.S. presidential election system is evolving toward what some characterize as perpetual campaigning. As a result, no one with any real power is—or has the time and energy to be—concerned about how things work. At least this was the judgment of many Americans at Oiso, including some deeply involved in politics.

Even if these obstacles to a thoughtful approach to policy did not exist, there is strong resistance in America to "industrial policy" or anything suggesting an intrusive, guiding governmental hand in the private sector. Despite some excellent work demonstrating the need for purposeful and assertive national policies,[2] there is public frustration with the dominant role of experts and officials and an almost ideological aversion to "Washington solutions."

One ought not, of course, exaggerate the qualities of the bureaucracy. By and large it is composed of talented and dedicated people. But they are no more immune than any other segment of society from limited knowledge and narrow perspectives, a tendency toward turf protection, and an inability to forecast the future. With their roles now reduced in many instances to managing and protecting existing programs rather than creating new ones, and under the conflicting political pressures alluded to above, their capacity for adopting a broad vision has not proven to be great.

As a result, "policy" is often the by-product of political and institutional confrontation between the President and the Congress, where the prudential brakes of expert and skeptical bureaucratic judgments are either weakened or simply eliminated. In many instances, the process is dominated by competitive catering to special interests or to swings in public mood. To state the obvious, policy toward Japan is not immune from these realities.

Just as we saw in the case of Japan, some people believe that, as American women are more proportionately employed, especially at responsible levels, their attitudes toward social concerns and "humaneness" may make for a kinder and gentler atmosphere in the workplace, perhaps blunting the sharp edge of international competition. But others believe that as more and more of these women become dissatisfied with their economic prospects because of unequal pay and inadequate promotion opportunities, they will take the threat to their interests from foreign competition more seriously and will become a force for greater confrontation with Japan, not less. Even now, American women employed by Japanese subsidiaries in the United States are filing lawsuits over alleged discrimination. Unless remedied, the stresses that sociologists see affecting American women broadly today—including the rising number of those who are responsible for managing low-income, single-parent households—will only intensify these antagonistic feelings.

A basic problem is America's consumption-oriented society, with its stress on short time horizons in respect to both corporate profits and individual savings. And despite a general recognition that the U.S. government must "do something" to resolve its financial plight—beyond juggling the books—thus far real results have proven hard to come by.

LOOKING AHEAD

So, on the one hand, we find that American and Japanese interests are importantly intertwined, and that our two societies have growing commonalities—encompassing not only shared interests and similar values but also parallel problems, such as the aging of our populations—that ought to make it easier and easier for us to understand, and get along with, one another. On the other hand, we see uncertainties in both our societies—about ourselves and about each other—that incline us either to be protective of our own, narrowly defined, well-being or to suspect the motives and objectives of the other, or both.

More Like Us—Flawed Assumptions

One could argue that Americans need to adjust their expectations and demands downward, while Japanese need to ratchet theirs up. Put so simply, however, this view obscures the underlying strength of the United States and the still diffident, if evolving, mind-set of the Japanese. But it does point to the changes in the *relative* roles the United States and Japan play in the world and their shifting power relationship.

The changes in attitudes required by these changing realities can only come about slowly. In the meantime, the increasingly judgmental finger pointing that is going on is particularly unproductive, not merely with respect to alleged specific instances of "unfairness" in trading practices but more generally about each other's failings. Despite the continuing high affinity each people has for the other, and the continuing mutual feelings of friendship and respect, more and more Japanese view Americans as self-indulgent, wasteful, undisciplined, racist, and demanding; they see the United States as unwilling to make a place for them in decision-making councils while it insists that Tokyo foot the bill. More and more Americans consider the Japanese unappreciative, mercantilistic, arrogant, racist, and irresponsible on social issues; they believe that Japan is unwilling to bear its fair share of the burden while it insists that Washington "understand" the special political and social circumstances that limit Japan's ability either to open certain sensitive markets or to contribute to resolution of problems far from its shores.

As the foregoing discussion suggests, and as the following chapters demonstrate with even greater forcefulness, many of these images have some basis in fact. But full-blown, they are caricatures that do little to advance our respective interests or to help resolve problems. Perhaps even more important, they inhibit the prospects for cooperation on a range of issues of vital importance to both countries and to the world at large.

The differences between Japan and the United States should not be minimized. The two societies start from very dissimilar foundations, what one Japanese at Oiso characterized as a conservative/nationalist base in Japan and a liberal/internationalist base in the United States. Moreover, it is likely that, within a context of some convergence in social attitudes and behavior, a pluralistic and individualistic pattern will remain dominant in the United States, while in Japan the emphasis on the group will prevail. Whether the measure is homogeneity, hours of work, diversity of life-style, management techniques, or emphasis on social justice versus economic efficiency, the twain will meet only in certain ways, and we will have to live with that reality.

Even on a practical level, numerous problems influence how the two societies can interact. Effective means of contact have not been developed, for example, between Japanese and the U.S. Congress or between Americans and the Diet. Obviously exceptions exist, but, as a general matter, both Japanese and Americans decry the lack of regular, long-term communication, seeing that which does exist largely as crisis-oriented and usually too late to be effective. (This is despite the explosion of lobbyists representing Japanese interests in Washington, who in fact may be so numerous that they create a negative effect.) In this connection, several people at Oiso emphasized the importance of understanding the political and social *process* in each country—rather than simply issues—as a key to managing the relationship. Still, this is difficult. Many Japanese see the United States as too vast and with too many actors to relate to easily, and Americans as too imperious to tolerate frank criticism; American complaints about Japan are often centered on the closedness of the process to outsiders.

The confrontation between principle and practice in times of hardship, cited earlier in terms of the limits on Americans' tolerance for domestic diversity, also applies to attitudes about Japanese investment in the United States. In a healthy economic climate a decade ago, Americans in and out of government leaned very hard on the Japanese to invest in the United States; if you are going to sell in our market, you must also manufacture here, the argument went. Now such investment is seen as more of a threat. When the Japanese are not accused of "buying up America," they are blamed for creating "excess capacity" in industry and of displacing less efficient American producers rather than expanding the pool of employment opportunities. A fear exists that in a global recession, Japanese firms will tend to close overseas plants—and lay off foreign workers—before cutting production at home. Moreover, the fact that many Japanese operations have been established in nonunion environments in the United States has led to recriminations by American unionists and politicians who had joined in encouraging that investment in years past. This raises questions about the long-term wisdom of the way in which Japanese firms deal with American unions and the risk they face of losing on the political front what they have gained in the market. It also raises interesting questions about the differences between Japanese and American unions, especially the former's generally positive attitudes toward flexible work rules and plant modernization, attitudes Japanese executives say they find alarmingly lacking in unionized American plants.

Japanese investors still find themselves ardently courted by U.S. state and local governments, but criticized when their inward-looking mode of operation creates problems in the communities where they establish themselves. The question of "good citizenship" has been compounded by racially insensitive statements by some leading politicians in Japan about American blacks and other minorities. The Japanese respond that the issue is not one of values but rather, as far as hiring practices are concerned, of survival, of employing those who are qualified to do the job and retaining those, including middle managers, who work hard and loyally rather than merely punch a time clock. They say that they recognize the need to adapt to some extent to the local environment and to be "socially responsible" but argue that, if they become totally "localized," they will lose their competitive advantage. Japanese companies are increasingly generous to local U.S. charities in an effort to demonstrate their goodwill, but, while some efforts are being made, the firms still tend to be reticent about direct participation in community activities. One wonders whether the Japanese understand that, however flawed actual performance by U.S. firms may be, in the American context it is important to be seen to be promoting social justice, not just abiding by it.

A major problem in addressing the issue of economic competition is the difference in corporate objectives. The Japanese are preoccupied with growth of the company and its market share over time, while Americans stress short-term profitability. It is arguable that such different perspectives are a direct function of the financial market system in each country, and that Americans should examine ways to lower the cost of capital. This is particularly pertinent in an era of leveraged buyouts, when time horizons shrink not to days or weeks, but to hours. The point for our purposes here is that this difference in perspectives and objectives generally leads to resentment and recriminations, where greater understanding might be more useful.

Lest they take too much satisfaction from this implicit criticism of American practices, Japanese should understand that they cannot expect to continue to enjoy open access to investment opportunities in the United States if such opportunities remain restricted in Japan. It is legitimate to ask whether the limitations, especially in the area of mergers and acquisitions, are not principally due to private-sector behavior rather than to government policy. In either case, however, the political reality is that the standard of reciprocity may well be increasingly invoked in determining American openness, even if its strict application would hurt American consumers as much as Japanese producers. As in the area of minority hiring, Americans tend to look not just at the stated intent of trade and investment rules but at results, as well.

The style of interaction between the two societies and governments is also of enormous importance. On the one hand, Japanese complain about excessive American pressure—"bashing," in the minds of many—saying this is an unacceptable way for two supposed equals to deal with one another and that its most important effect is to generate mutual hostility and, intertwined with healthy national pride, a certain degree of pugnacious nationalistic resentment. At the same time, many Japanese, including some of the same people who complain, say that without external pressure, nothing would change in Japan. Many, therefore, welcome or even invite it. How to cope with this dilemma is not self-evident, but it is clear that there must be movement away from the past—and current—pattern of reliance on American pressure to force changes on Japan that Japanese want or should make anyway in their own self-interest.

Political Leadership

This brings us back to the issue of political leadership. Special interests in both countries cannot be expected to take a broader perspective and to make changes "for the sake of the relationship." But governments have an obligation to do just that, and to refrain from simply pandering to parochial pleading. Making the necessary adjustments is certainly not going to be easy for either government, particularly because the time for doing so is limited—the political mood in each country is becoming too sour for delay. The difficulty is increased by the fact that each country appears to underestimate the other, and that neither leadership seems to grasp the seriousness of the problem.

Perhaps, as suggested earlier, many aspects of science and technology, and of the relationship itself, are too vast, and changing too rapidly, for governments to control. But governments do have choices about the legal and regulatory environment they create, for example, for fostering competitiveness, and about the priorities they set and the attitudes they convey.

Facing Reality—Attitudes Do Count

Surely not all of the problems are ones of attitudes and values. The harsh reality of the unbalanced trade accounts exists, and whoever is to "blame," that reality has political implications in both countries. And as observed earlier, the point is *not* whether our societies are "converging." (In fact, while some structural convergence is under way, it is taking place between enduringly unique cultures. In any case, it is not realistic to think we would necessarily have a smoother relationship if we were more alike; similarity carries no such guarantee.)

The point *is* that, while attitudes are not everything, they do count. It is true that Japanese do not look on an unfettered free market in the same way that Americans do—or at least they have not done so historically. Yet one of the key conclusions to be drawn from Professor Shimada's analysis is that, however slow it may be, the increasing globalization of the Japanese economy—with its increased exposure to heterogeneous cultures, values, and social systems, and with the reduced level of both governmental control and the protection it involves—will make the Japanese people and corporations more aware of the richness and complexity of such other cultures and institutions, and more open to accommodation with them. Even at a time of seeming dominance by Japan in certain technologies and manufacturing techniques, farsighted observers there see the rigidity of the Japanese system and way of thinking as leading to a competitive decline that will be far more profound than any problems trade restraints from the outside world could create.

Similarly, Americans are beginning to understand that the fundamental problems in our economy lie at home—in our savings and investment rates; our fiscal profligacy; our neglect of the things that government and business can do together to enhance competitiveness even within a nonindustrial policy environment; and our education, poverty, and drug crises—and that our solutions must be found at home, as well. Moreover, the fact that others may frame issues differently from the way we do does not necessarily mean they are wrong.

As we examine the relationship, we find that each society has much to learn from the other, and is beginning to do so. Interdependence is growing not only on the political/security side of the equation and not only in trade of physical goods, but also in the form of a "strategic" economic alliance represented by the two-way exchange of high technology, the increasing number of joint ventures, and the exploding levels of capital flows (see Eleanor Westney, chapter 4).

The plain fact is that the United States and Japan need each other, and if people can be brought to recognize the broad community of interests between our governments and societies, then handling the problems and creating new cooperative ventures will be considerably easier. Among other things, the relationship requires a lot more mutual respect, including in what we say and how we say it. Americans need to understand the feelings of vulnerability that persist in Japan despite its rise to economic superpower status and, indeed, the very real pain and dislocation caused by the structural adjustment that has resulted in part from American demands. Japanese not only must be more sensitive to social realities in the United States, but they also need to appreciate that some of America's current problems derive from a past willingness both to tolerate and to contribute actively to the growth of other nations, most particularly including Japan, behind a wall of favorable terms that were of some cost to the

United States. Moreover, while the United States is no exception to the reality that national policies are—or, anyway, should be—designed to promote national interests, Americans have understood the importance to their own well-being of benefiting and protecting others; this is not an approach widely appreciated in Japan, and certainly not one Japan has adopted for itself.[3] Each side needs to face the reality that, like itself, the other has political constraints. But neither can afford to simply let those forces dominate policy, however powerful they may be.

A complicating factor in finding positive approaches is the media in both countries, concentrating as they quite naturally do on problem areas and confrontation rather than on "success stories" and cooperation. What one can or should do about that in free societies is not immediately clear. But one ought not underestimate the negative impact of, for example, the U.S. media attention to the so-called revisionist writers on U.S.–Japan relations[4] and of Japanese correspondents' and columnists' fixation on every disagreement and criticism as a sign of crisis.

Suggestions have been made, even at Oiso, that there should be a diminishing of the relationship in order to permit a cooling of tension; if we are less important to each other, the argument goes, then our problems will not matter so much. But this is not realistic, nor desirable. Consider the costs to the United States of less economic cooperation—including a slower flow of Japanese capital that finances our deficit and of sophisticated goods that not only fill our homes but constitute vital components for our high-technology industries and our military systems. Consider the costs to Japan of being cut adrift in a world suspicious of its intentions and its capabilities, and of being denied essential markets in the United States. Consider, too, the consequences for peace and stability in Asia and beyond of diminishing or terminating U.S.–Japan security cooperation.

Not only can bilateral relations act as a catalyst for domestic change, but domestic change has a crucial impact on bilateral relations. A central task for both countries is to harness and promote that change in positive ways, defusing the ill feelings and complications that are bound to arise in such a rich and complex relationship, and promoting our mutual benefit. To say that Japan is not experienced as a world leader or that the United States lacks the structure and the incentive to do long-term planning is simply not good enough. Both sides need to accept the requirement of looking beyond their present roles and styles of operation. Each needs to do better—better at facing its own shortcomings, better at understanding the other's internal dynamics, better at communicating, and better at seeing challenges as opportunities rather than as threats.

NOTES

1. Elliott Abrams, "Panama: How America Lost Its Will to Act," *The Washington Post*, October 15, 1989, p. B1.
2. See, for example, President's Commission on Industrial Competitiveness, *Global Competitiveness: The New Reality* (Washington, D.C., 1985).
3. The expansion of Japan's aid program is important and welcome. But the program's terms are still restricted, and much of the recent increase reflects changes in exchange rates rather than the devoting of a substantially greater proportion of national wealth for that purpose. Moreover, the growth in aid has largely been imposed on the public by the government, a measure that is praiseworthy as an exercise in leadership, but of some concern as we begin to see signs of public resistance to the program's further expansion.
4. Several of those writers focus on the fundamental problems in American society and government, which is all to the good. But the media generally focus on their sometimes flawed descriptions of how Japan is "different" and their questionable prescriptions for restrictive trade policies toward Japan, thus feeding the protectionist mood in the Congress and beyond.

2

RECENT CHANGES IN AMERICAN SOCIAL ATTITUDES

Howard Schuman

She said to me early in the afternoon, "What is the answer?" I was
silent. "In that case," she said, "What is the question?"

Alice B. Toklas, *What Is Remembered*

When we speak not only of Japan and America as nations, but of
Japanese and Americans as peoples who must meet and deal
with one another, then their distinctive attitudes become important to understand. Where social attitudes are similar and are
moving in the same direction, communication and mutual understanding should be relatively easy. Where attitudes or their
direction—or pace—of change differ in important ways, mis-
communication or even conflict is more likely.[1]

In this chapter we examine recent changes in some key
American social attitudes. Although the focus is on change, the
very act of singling out certain attitudes to describe is itself a
significant step, since some of these attitudes are unlikely to be
equally important for a Japanese social scientist describing Japanese attitudes. Thus, as in many other contexts, the questions
posed may be as important as the answers given.

CHANGES IN RACIAL ATTITUDES

One of the most critical attitudes in America, and one that is
much studied, is ordinarily distant from Japan and from Japanese concerns: that of majority groups toward minorities. Unlike
most countries, and certainly unlike Japan, the United States
contains a mixture of many immigrant peoples, predominantly
European in origin, but now, and increasingly, African, Latin
American, and Asian (including Japanese-American) as well. We

will not deal generally with this extraordinary heterogeneity, but only with a line that has divided the population over almost its entire history: that between blacks and whites.

Fifty years ago, racial minorities received little national attention in the United States, and much of the white population took for granted segregation and the profoundly inferior status of blacks. As Figure 1 shows, in the early 1940s the majority of white Americans accepted racial segregation in schools and even open discrimination against blacks in employment opportunities. For example, in 1942 only about 30 percent of a national white sample believed that white and black children should go to the same schools, and in 1944 only 45 percent believed that black people deserved an equal opportunity to compete for jobs. Figure 1 also shows, however, that from the 1940s onward, acceptance of the principles of integration and equal treatment regardless of race has grown steadily, a trend that has not halted even in recent years.[2]

In addition, Figure 1 shows the trend in attitudes about one of the most sensitive racial issues, that of black-white intermarriage. Although the levels of white support on this issue are much lower than those regarding employment and schools, we see the same basic upward movement. Moreover, the fact that *levels* of support differ among these issues provides some evidence that the responses represent expressions of genuine attitudes: if respondents were giving only lip-service answers to please interviewers, it would have been equally easy to support racial integration on all three questions.

A problem often raised about data like those in Figure 1 is whether they also reflect changes in behavior. Of course, it would be foolish to expect a completely consistent relationship between verbal responses and other behavior—in surveys or in any other sphere of life. But anyone who has lived through or studied carefully the past half-century of American history will be aware of immense changes in race-related behavior. For example, the U.S. Army was completely segregated until 1948; now, not only is it substantially integrated, but a black general rose to become President Reagan's primary personal adviser on foreign affairs

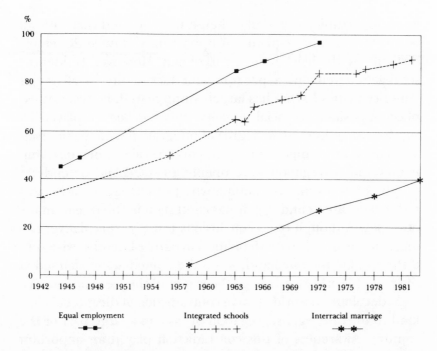

Source: For the actual percentages and their sources, see Howard Schuman, Charlotte
    Steeh, and Lawrence Bobo, *Racial Attitudes in America: Trends and Interpretations*
    (Cambridge, Mass.: Harvard University Press, 1985).

FIG. 1.   WHITE AMERICANS FAVORING EQUAL EMPLOYMENT FOR WHITES
        AND BLACKS, RACIALLY INTEGRATED SCHOOLS, AND
            INTERRACIAL MARRIAGE (*by year*)

and then Chairman of the Joint Chiefs of Staff, the highest
military position in the nation. And despite a great deal of de
facto residential segregation, many previously all-white middle-
class communities now have some black residents. More generally, the very change in norms that makes some prejudiced
responses "socially undesirable" constrains many other forms of
white behavior to be egalitarian in a way that was not true several
decades ago.[3] Indeed, it might be better to characterize the
change that has occurred as a change in norms, rather than in
attitudes.

Racial division in the United States is not disappearing; far
from it. Much controversy surrounds questions of how much the
federal government should press for integration and how much
extra effort should be made to create equality of outcome as well

as of opportunity, especially when it is recognized that without government action, equality of opportunity may be extremely difficult for the black minority to obtain. Moreover, residential segregation remains a predominant fact of life in all major American cities.[4] What has largely disappeared, however, is explicit opposition to racial equality; this has been replaced by support for at least some degree of integration, and that in itself is a significant change from several decades ago, when discrimination and segregation were openly accepted and defended.[5]

It is interesting to examine why this change in racial attitudes came about and why it has continued in the face of many obstacles. Although one's conclusions must be speculative, two major forces are clear, both political in nature but otherwise very different. On the one hand, when the United States claimed at the end of World War II to be the leader of the free and increasingly decolonized world, it was a contradiction of the most blatant kind to tolerate legal segregation by race in a large part of the country. Awareness of this contradiction played an important role in mobilizing the more informed parts of the population to question traditional racial norms. At the same time, the movement of blacks from the rural South into cities and, especially, into the urban North created a black population much less passive in accepting racist norms and increasingly able to carry political weight in elections. In fact, a number of white political leaders in the Deep South today owe their positions in part to black votes, and this certainly makes a difference in what goes on in government at every level in the country.

The homogeneity of the Japanese population, its lack of a large visible minority, and its different role in the world (at least until recently) has made this issue, so fundamental to American society, much less salient in Japan. Their nation's very different history has sometimes led to insensitive statements by Japanese leaders, who do not recognize the degree to which invidious characterizations of ethnic and racial minorities are unacceptable in American public life. Equally important, Japanese-owned companies in the United States are sometimes perceived as discriminatory in their hiring practices or, where not overtly discriminatory, as unhelpful in contributing to the employment and training of minorities, which is essential to the United States at this time.

THE ROLE OF WOMEN

Although the most visible social movement of the past half-century was to end the segregation of America's largest minority, at least equally important has been a movement to change the status of an American majority, namely, women. Efforts in this direction go back many years, certainly to the women's suffrage movement in the early part of the century. But this most recent attempt at fundamental change is usually dated from around 1970, and it has proceeded fairly rapidly since then. Unlike changes in racial attitudes, shifts in gender attitudes appear to be occurring in Japan also, and they are being monitored by surveys. Thus, the difference between the two countries in this case is one of starting points and pace, with changes in the United States being ahead of those in Japan, no doubt in part because the subordination of women was less extreme in America than in traditional Japan.

Figure 2 shows results on the quite general question of whether women are "now looked on with more respect as individual human beings": the proportions of men and women agreeing in 1985 were half again the 1975 levels. Moreover, the trends appear to be much the same for men and for women, an important finding that is generally true for gender attitudes. (By contrast, black and white attitudes on racial issues are more sharply separated; for example, approval by blacks of school integration has been close to 100 percent since first asked of blacks in 1972, and black approval of intermarriage has been over 75 percent; the percentages for whites, reported earlier, are much lower.) Figure 2 also shows data for as early as 1938 on a question about whether a woman should be able to earn money "in business or industry if she has a husband capable of supporting her." In 1938, only some 20 percent of the population approved of remunerated work by women, but the proportion now is 80 percent, obviously a huge change. (The earliest proportion

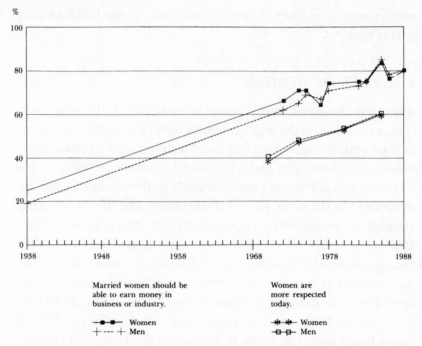

%

Married women should be
able to earn money in
business or industry.

━■━■━ Women
+ --- + Men

Women are
more respected
today.

━*━*━ Women
━❏━❏━ Men

Sources: The 1938 data on married women working are from the Gallup Organization,
Princeton, N.J.; the other years are from James Allen Davis and Tom W. Smith,
General Social Survey, 1972–1988 (Chicago: National Opinion Research Center,
1988); all reported by Rita J. Simon and Jean M. Landis, "The Polls—A Report:
Women's and Men's Attitudes about Woman's Place and Role," *Public Opinion
Quarterly* 53 (Summer 1989), pp. 265–276.

FIG. 2.   AMERICAN MEN AND WOMEN AGREEING WITH TWO
STATEMENTS REGARDING WOMEN'S ROLES, *by year*

may have been held down somewhat by the effects of the Great
Depression, but a large change clearly has occurred and, as
Figure 2 shows, has continued into the 1980s. Also notable is the
small drop from 1985 to 1986, which is statistically reliable and
may indicate that a plateau has been reached.)

Figure 3 shows increases in *disagreement* with statements
claiming that men are better suited for politics than women, and
that a wife should give preference to her husband's career over
her own. The trends are basically in the same direction as in the
previous figure, and, although not shown in detail, there is again
no large or systematic difference in responses by men and by
women.

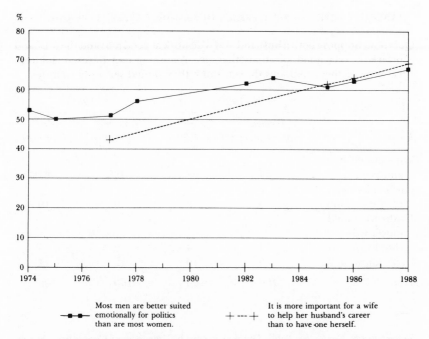

Source: James Allen Davis and Tom W. Smith, *General Social Survey, 1972–1988* (Chicago: National Opinion Research Center, 1988).

FIG. 3.   AMERICANS DISAGREEING WITH TWO STATEMENTS ABOUT
WOMEN IN POLITICS AND WOMEN'S CAREERS (*by year*)

However, the apparent high level of support for a woman's career vis-à-vis her husband's does not hold nearly as well when a more concrete and difficult dilemma is presented. Thus, the Roper Organization asked the question about moving for a better job and obtained the results indicated in Table 1. When the issue is posed in this way, most Americans—and women even more than men—believe that the wife should follow her husband's lead. Despite some decrease over the five-year period, the proportion giving preference to the husband's job remains the majority. This finding is confirmed when the question is reversed and it is the wife who has the opportunity to move to a better job: only 20 percent and 22 percent, respectively, of women and men in 1985 said the man should quit his job and relocate with his wife. Thus, one must be careful not to confuse the shape of long-term trends in generalized attitudes over time with attitudes toward related but more sharply focused issues at

TABLE 1. WIFE'S CAREER VERSUS HUSBAND'S CAREER, 1980 AND 1985

Question: Suppose both a husband and wife work at good jobs and the husband is offered a very good job in another city. Assuming they have no children, which one of these solutions do you think they should seriously consider?

	1980		1985	
Answer	Women (N=3,007)	Men (N=1,004)	Women (N=3,000)	Men (N=1,000)
Wife should quit and relocate	77%	68%	72%	62%
Husband should turn down job	10	18	10	19
Husband should move, wife should stay	4	4	6	5
Don't know, other	9	10	12	14
Total	100	100	100	100

Source: Roper Center for Public Opinion Research, University of Connecticut, Storrs, 1980 and 1985.

any particular point in time, since the percentages in the latter case depend on the specific circumstances the question presents. General support for a wife's career drops sharply when the dilemma is concretized in the Roper question on who should give up their job when one spouse must do so.[6]

Changes in attitudes toward the role of women appear to be occurring in Japan that are similar in kind and direction to those in the United States. It seems that the status of women is still much more subordinate in Japan than in the United States, but relevant survey questions that would allow precise documentation of this point do not seem to have been asked identically in the two countries.[7]

MARRIAGE AND SEXUAL RELATIONS

Changed views of the occupational roles of married women have obvious implications for the nature of marriage and of family life; indeed, some see the development of careers for women as a threat to the whole basis of marriage. However, acceptance of separate careers for women should not be taken to mean that the proportion of young Americans who prefer to remain single has greatly increased. Most American high school seniors (70–80 percent) indicate a clear desire to marry, and at least over the past decade or so these figures have not changed, though the preferred age for marriage has risen somewhat for both sexes. What does seem to have changed is that negative views toward those who remain single are now less widespread than they once were. In addition, over the past several decades divorce has become much more acceptable, though during the 1980s support seems to have leveled off or even to have decreased slightly.

Two questions about sexual relations outside of marriage indicate how the ideal conception of marriage itself has been altered, although not in quite as fundamental a way as is sometimes assumed. Figure 4 shows substantial liberalization between the early 1970s and 1988 in attitudes toward sex before marriage, but a decrease in acceptance of extramarital sex. Premarital sex is now completely approved by about 40 percent of the population, but similar complete approval for extramarital sex reaches only about 3 percent, and the more qualified approval shown in Figure 4 has dropped from around 15 percent to about 10 percent. The implication of this change is that sex itself is decreasingly seen as being associated only with marriage, but fidelity within marriage is still highly valued. (Responses to a slightly different question in the mid-1960s suggest that the proportion approving of extramarital sex had earlier increased by some six percentage points to reach the 15 percent figure in 1973 shown in Figure 4, but if so the subsequent decline has been equally great.) Again, these responses reflect attitudes not behavior, but they represent important social values and they provide some normative constraint on actions. Taken as a whole, the evidence suggests that conceptions of marriage and marriage roles have changed considerably, but that marriage as a unique and exclusive bonding remains highly valued and highly sought.[8]

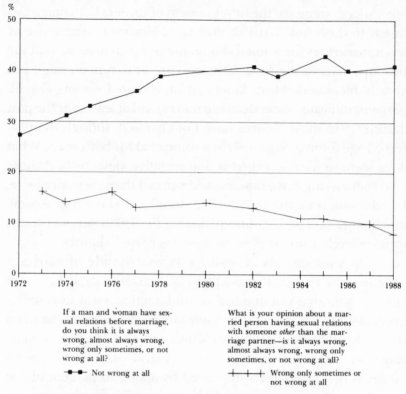

Source: James Allen Davis and Tom W. Smith, *General Social Survey, 1972–1988* (Chicago: National Opinion Research Center, 1988).

FIG. 4. AMERICANS AGREEING WITH TWO STATEMENTS
ABOUT SEX AND MARRIAGE (*by year*)

CHILD-REARING VALUES

Another area in which basic values are reflected is child-rearing. A question asked in the metropolitan Detroit area in 1958, 1971, and 1983 required adults to rank five possible values for a child to learn: to obey; to be well liked or popular; to think for himself; to work hard; and to help others when in need.[9] Our interest here is in the two values that have shown the most change over time: to obey, which emphasizes traditional conformity, and to think for himself, which emphasizes the child's development of autonomy.[10] Figure 5 shows the preference of the population in each survey for a child's autonomy rather than obedience. The proportion choosing the former over the latter rose from 65

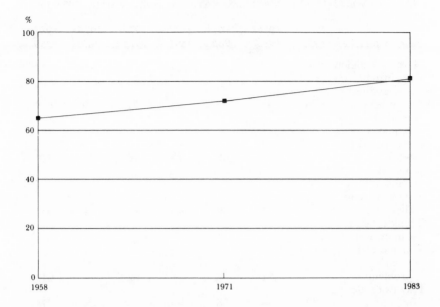

Source: Duane F. Alwin, "Religion and Parental Child-rearing Orientations: Evidence of a Catholic-Protestant Convergence," *American Journal of Sociology* 92 (1986), pp. 412–440.

FIG. 5.   ADULTS WHO PREFER CHILDREN TO BE MORE AUTONOMOUS
THAN OBEDIENT, DETROIT, 1958, 1971, 1983

percent in 1958 to 71 percent in 1971, and then to 81 percent in 1983.

Other evidence suggests that the 1958 figure was already considerably higher than would have been obtained two or three decades earlier. It is less certain that the proportion has continued to grow since 1983, and the available evidence suggests a plateau. In any case, however, over the past several decades the valuation of autonomy for children has risen noticeably. At least part of this change is probably due to increasing levels of education in the United States, since the choice of autonomy over conformity is associated with greater education; but other, less easily isolated factors are probably involved as well.

RELIGION

Trends on a number of traditional religious attachments and beliefs are presented in Table 2.[11] Most of the questions show

TABLE 2. PERCENTAGE OF AMERICAN ADULTS MAINTAINING VARIOUS
RELIGIOUS BELIEFS AND PRACTICES, NATIONAL SURVEY DATA, 1952–1985

Belief or practice	1952–1955	1956–1960	1961–1965	1966–1970	1971–1975	1976–1980	1981–1985
Have no religion	—	2	—	3	—	8	8*
Are church/synagogue members	73	—	73	—	71	69	68*
Attended religious services last week	48	48	46	43	40	41	41*
Consider religion very important in their lives	75	—	70	—	—	54	56*
Think religion can answer all or most of today's problems	—	81	—	—	62	—	61*
Pray twice a day or more	39	—	38	—	—	24	27*
Believe in God as a. universal spirit	98	97	97	98	—	94	95*
Believe that Bible is actual word of God to be taken literally	—	—	65	—	—	39	38*
Believe in life after death	77	74	75	73	69	69	71*
Believe Jesus Christ is God	74	—	72	—	—	—	70*
Believe in heaven	72	—	68	—	—	71	—
Believe in hell	—	—	54	—	—	53	—

Sources: The "no religion" percentages are from Glenn, "The Trend in 'No Religion' Respondents in U.S. National Surveys, Late 1950s to Early 1980s," *Public Opinion Quarterly* 51 (1987), pp. 293–314; all other percentages are from the Gallup Organization, *Religion in America, 50 Years: 1935–1985*, Gallup Report, No. 238 (Princeton, N.J., 1985a). All percentages were calculated with "no opinion" and similar responses included in the base. Table adapted from: Norval D. Glenn, "Social Trends in the United States: Evidence from Sample Surveys," *Public Opinion Quarterly* 51 (1987), pp. S109–S126.

—=Question not asked during this time period.

* Is significantly different from the first percentage in the series at least at the 0.05 level (two-tailed test).

Note: For time periods in which a question was asked more than once, the reported percentage is the mean of the results from the different surveys.

statistically significant declines from the 1950s into the 1980s. For example, the proportion of Americans for whom religion is very important in their lives decreased from 75 percent to 56 percent over the three decades, though little evidence of change can be noted during the most recent years. Belief in the Bible as the literal word of God declined by some 27 percentage points during just two decades. Some other changes illustrated in the table are less dramatic, but almost every comparison reveals some downward movement in claims of religious belief or behavior. Thus, despite the attention that religious fundamentalism has received in America in recent years, traditional religion seems to have less hold on the population than it did several decades ago. These results are consistent with most of the other changes noted so far—for example, decreasing emphasis on conformity on the part of children.

SOME INTERPRETATIONS OF THE TRENDS

Let us stop now and consider what larger interpretations can be offered for the changes we have reviewed.

Liberal or Conservative Direction?

Contrary to the impression that the most recent American presidential campaign may have created, most of these attitude changes—and some we have not considered, such as in the broad area of civil liberties—would probably be classified more as liberal than conservative in direction.[12] This is most obvious in the cases of racial and gender issues, but it also applies to child-rearing values, attitudes toward premarital sex, and decreasing belief in traditional religious doctrines. In a number of cases the changes appear to have leveled off during the 1980s, and some have even undergone slight reversals. For now, however, little evidence justifies the conclusion of a large and widespread reversal of earlier trends.

It would be a mistake, however, to assume that similar shifts have occurred in all areas that tend to divide liberals and conservatives in America. For example, Figure 6 shows that a lessening of support for capital punishment during the 1950s and 1960s

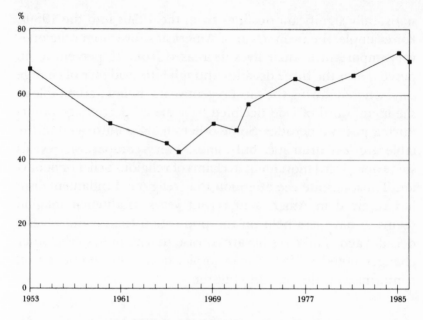

Source: The Gallup Organization, *The Gallup Report*, No. 244–245 (Princeton, N.J., January–February 1986), p. 12.

FIG. 6.   AMERICAN ADULTS FAVORING THE DEATH PENALTY
FOR MURDER, 1953–1985

has been succeeded by even higher support for it in the 1970s and 1980s. And we saw that, at least in recent years, rejection of extramarital sexual relations has increased. In the economic sphere, belief that the government "should do everything possible to improve the standard of living of all poor Americans" has decreased significantly: the drop over the past decade that can be documented is about ten percentage points, and comparison with data from the mid-1960s Great Society period probably would show an even steeper decline.

Overall, the available attitude survey data reveal no single grand political trend, but, if anything, as indicated earlier, on balance there has been more movement in a liberal than conservative direction, especially if viewed over the past several decades rather than just the last few years.

An obvious question is whether the same can be said for Japan and, more generally, whether there is evidence of a convergence in social values between the two countries. One senses that some convergence is occurring, but how real and how great it is cannot be determined without studies designed for careful comparison of both stated values and observable behavior, rather than rapid reviews of noncomparable data on an ad hoc basis.

A Growth of Individualism?

A more general argument that has recently attracted attention in the United States is that many of the changes we have reviewed reflect a growth of individualism, both expressive (meaning a preoccupation with personal fulfillment) and utilitarian (meaning materialistic), with a consequent loss of traditional commitment to the community and to civic responsibility.[13] Somewhat similar issues have also been raised in Japan about its younger generation.

It is useful to note that our survey starting points are relatively recent, whereas questions about American individualism go back at least to Tocqueville's Democracy in America (1840): "Individualism is a calm and considered feeling which disposes each citizen to isolate himself from the mass of his fellows and withdraw into the circle of family and friends; with this little society formed to his taste, he gladly leaves the greater society to look after itself."[14] Here we can address only the question of whether individualism and its presumed consequences seem to have grown stronger in the United States over the past few years.

Some obvious aspects of increased individualism in an expressive sense seem evident in several of our results. If children are being urged "to think for themselves," rather than simply to conform to adult wishes, that is individualistic almost by definition. From another standpoint, support for premarital sex can be regarded as individualistic in terms of personal gratification, although it may sometimes be justified as a way of reducing the likelihood of too early marriage. More indirectly, the increasing acceptance of careers for women is often phrased in terms of individual fulfillment, as against a more purely supportive role within a traditional family structure. One should also acknowledge the widespread use of drugs of various sorts as representing what might be considered an extreme, perhaps pathological, form of individualism.

Recent data are also available on attitudes toward individualism in the sense of materialism. Figure 7 shows that the importance of making money has been growing among representative samples of high school seniors. Yet at the same time, the proportion of adults who say they would continue to work even if this were not necessary for financial reasons has been increasing (not shown). And, as Figure 8 indicates, self-reported charitable and social service activities are on the rise. Thus, these somewhat scattered findings are mixed on the issue of recent changes in a materialistic direction.

When we turn to claims that individualism means the loss of attachment to larger institutions and to the community, the argument becomes a little less clear. Certainly the meaning of marriage changes when premarital sex and cohabitation are approved and when divorce is accepted as a quite legitimate

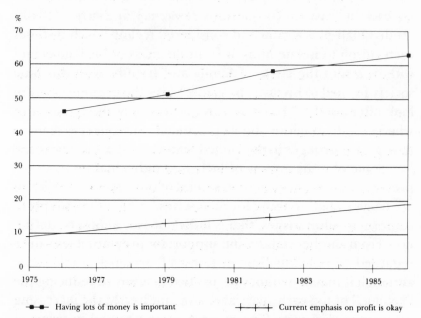

—■—■— Having lots of money is important   —+—+—+— Current emphasis on profit is okay

Source: Jerald G. Bachman, Lloyd D. Johnston, and Patrick M. O'Malley, *Monitoring the Future: Questionnaire Responses from the Nation's High School Seniors* (Ann Arbor, Michigan: Institute for Social Research, University of Michigan, 1975–1987).

FIG. 7.   AMERICAN HIGH SCHOOL SENIORS AGREEING WITH TWO
STATEMENTS ABOUT THE IMPORTANCE OF MONEY, 1975–1986

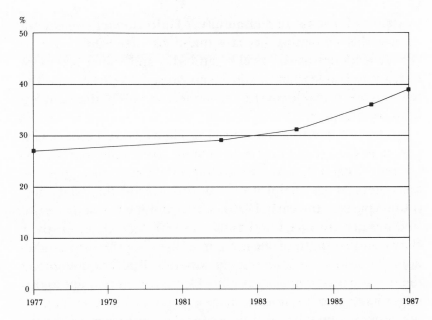

Source: The Gallup Organization, The Gallup Report, No. 262 (Princeton, N.J., July 1987), p. 33.

FIG. 8.   AMERICAN ADULTS REPORTING INVOLVEMENT IN CHARITY OR SOCIAL SERVICE ACTIVITIES, 1977–1987

solution to an unhappy marriage. However, the fact that most Americans still desire to be married and that the marital commitment is regarded by most, at least ideally, as precluding other sexual partners suggests that it is much too early to see the marriage bond itself losing its importance in America.

Still, as the Tocqueville quotation suggested, even increased concern with marriage and family could be consistent with a kind of individualism that is devoted to personal happiness without regard for the larger community beyond the family. The growth of cities and new suburbs and most other ongoing changes in living arrangements, transportation, and communications certainly indicate that the self-contained small community of America's distant past is less prominent today. At the same time, the previous figure on charitable activities and other data on the proliferation of various types of voluntary organizations seem somewhat inconsistent with assumptions about the disappearance of a sense of community.[15] Unfortunately we cannot resolve this ambiguity because questions that would give us clearer evidence at the level of attitudes and values are more difficult to frame than the questions presented earlier, and the few that are available cover quite limited periods of time and are hard to interpret.

The two questions addressed in Figure 9 are perhaps tangential to the issue of how individualism affects the community, but they suggest that Americans today do not, in the aggregate, see others as less helpful or less trustworthy than did their counterparts in the early 1970s. These and the previous several findings are advanced hesitantly and with little claim for their clarity and strength of meaning in addressing the dire predictions about loss of community in America. But they are among the few systematic indicators available that seem relevant to this larger issue, and it is notable at least that, taken as a set, they do not provide unequivocal support for the most extreme predictions.

POSTSCRIPT ON AMERICAN ATTITUDES TOWARD JAPAN

This chapter has focused on changes in American social attitudes that are important to understand in any comparison with Japan. It is also interesting to examine American attitudes toward Japan itself. One important American annual survey has been asking such questions about a number of countries for the past decade and a half. In 1988, 73 percent of a national sample used the top (more positive) five points on a ten-point scale to describe Japan. This compares with 97 percent for Canada, the highest-ranked of all countries; 46 percent for the Soviet Union, the lowest-ranked; and 71 percent for China, the country ranked closest to Japan on this scale. It is also of note that Americans' attitude toward Japan, as measured by this scale, has stayed about the same over the last several years, whereas their esteem of some other countries has either risen (for example, the USSR) or fallen (for example, Israel).[16]

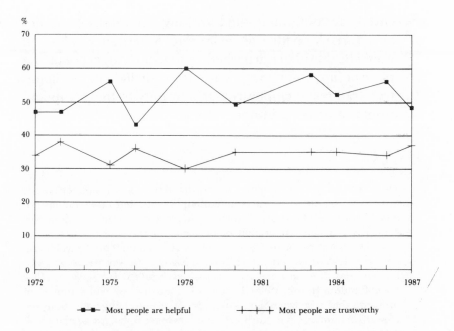

Source: James Allen Davis and Tom W. Smith, *General Social Survey, 1972–1988* (Chicago: National Opinion Research Center, 1988).

FIG. 9. AMERICAN ADULTS WHO BELIEVE THAT MOST PEOPLE ARE HELPFUL AND TRUSTWORTHY, 1972–1987

IMPLICATIONS

Finally, can one draw out of the findings any conclusions for U.S.–Japan relations? The opening chapter looks at that question on a broad basis. Here one can highlight three points of particular significance in terms of attitudes:

- The whole area of attitudes toward minorities is one where greater Japanese knowledge of—and sensitivity to—the American scene will be important to relations between the two countries.

- Although the starting point and pace of change differ significantly, the role of women in the two societies is evolving in the same direction, suggesting that in this dimension the two countries are not on a collision course.[17]

- Given the continuing—and growing—emphasis on autonomy (versus obedience) in raising American children, it would be useful to learn whether similar changes are taking place in Japan—and with what effect—in light of that country's traditional emphasis on conformity to the group and responsiveness to authority.

NOTES

1. The term "attitude" is used here as shorthand for not only opinions in the pro/con sense, but also beliefs, intentions, values, and other similar notions. There are, of course, a number of sources of error in attitude survey data. For a detailed treatment of problems in carrying out surveys of attitudes, as well as for references to other relevant methodological literature, see Howard Schuman and Graham Kalton, "Survey Methods," in G. Lindzey and E. Aronsen, eds., *Handbook on Social Psychology,* vol. 1 (New York: Random House, 1985). In addition, for a discussion of a number of problems that arise when the focus is specifically on change over time, see Howard Schuman, Charlotte Steeh, and Lawrence Bobo, *Racial Attitudes in America: Trends and Interpretations* (Cambridge, Mass.: Harvard University Press, 1985), ch. 2.
2. Most of the recent change has occurred through replacement of older cohorts by younger ones, whereas much of the earlier change (e.g., during the 1960s) also involved substantial shifting of individual attitudes throughout the age range. See Schuman et al., *Racial Attitudes,* pp. 127–135.
3. The issue is not really one of "attitudes versus actions," as it is often phrased, for the same inconsistencies occur between one action and another. A president may appoint a black person to a cabinet position, yet then defend tax-supported segregated schools, which may seem radically inconsistent to some. No single behavior, whether verbal *or* nonverbal, is necessarily linked to another in political affairs or in ordinary life.
4. See Reynolds Farley and Walter R. Allen, *The Color Line and the Quality of Life in America* (New York: Russell Sage Foundation, 1987).
5. See Schuman et al., *Racial Attitudes.*
6. It is quite possible as well that equalitarian responses to the more concrete question have also risen over time, albeit at a much lower level than for the generalized question; however, we lack data to demonstrate this. Much of the data in this section is reported in Rita J. Simon and Jean M. Lendia, "Women's and Men's Attitudes About a Woman's Place and Role," *Public Opinion Quarterly* 53 (1989), pp. 265–276.
7. See Susan Chira, "Working Women Find Slow Progress in Japan," *The New York Times,* December 4, 1988.
8. Data for this section come from Arland Thornton, "Changing Attitudes Towards Family Issues in the United States," *Journal of Marriage and the Family* 51 (1989), pp. 873–894. My interpretation, however, is somewhat different from Thornton's.

9. Although figures for metropolitan Detroit cannot be generalized to the nation, other comparisons indicate that they are not far off and that basic trends can certainly be generalized.

10. Experiments with other questions suggest that changing "himself" to "herself" is unlikely to alter the results in any appreciable way.

11. For recent views on trends in religious attitudes and beliefs that express doubts as to their decline, see Andrew Greeley, *Religious Change in America* (Cambridge, Mass.: Harvard University Press, 1989); and Robert Wuthnow, *The Restructuring of American Religion* (Princeton, N.J.: Princeton University Press, 1988).

12. See also Tom W. Smith, "Liberal and Conservative Trends in the United States since World War II," *Public Opinion Quarterly* (forthcoming, 1990).

13. Robert N. Bellah et al., *Habits of the Heart* (Berkeley: University of California Press, 1985); and Norval D. Glenn, "Social Trends in the United States: Evidence from Sample Surveys," *Public Opinion Quarterly* 51 (1987), pp. S109–S126,

14. Tocqueville, Alexis de, *Democracy in America*, vol. 2 (New York: Doubleday Anchor, [1840] 1969), p. 506.

15. For data on voluntary organizations in America see Frank R. Baumgartner and Jack C. Walker, "Survey Research and Membership in Voluntary Associations," *American Journal of Political Science* 32 (1988), pp. 908–923. For a contrary view, see Tom W. Smith, "Trends in Voluntary Group Membership: Comments on Baumgartner and Walker," *American Journal of Political Science* (forthcoming, 1990).

16. These results are from James Allen Davis and Tom W. Smith, *General Social Surveys, 1972–1988* (Chicago: National Opinion Research Center, 1988). Note that the data on China were obtained prior to spring 1989 and would probably be different if obtained today. A national survey conducted by *The New York Times* and CBS News six times over the past five years recently showed a decline in "generally friendly" feelings for Japan. From a high of 87 percent in July 1985 when the question was first asked, the favorable response dropped to a relatively steady 73–76 percent between May 1987 and June 1989. It then dropped again to 67 percent in mid-January 1990, as reported by Michael Oreskes, "Poll Detects Erosion of Positive Attitudes Toward Japan Among Amercians," *The New York Times*, February 6, 1990, p. B7. Whether this drop has long-term implications remains to be seen, but it is statistically significant.

17. For more detailed data on attitudes toward women's roles in the United States, see Karen O. Mason and Yu-Hsia Lu, "Attitudes Toward Women's Familial Roles: Changes in the United States, 1977–1985," *Gender and Society* 2, no. 1 (1988), pp. 39–57; and Karen O. Mason, John L. Czajka, and Sara Arber, "Change in U.S. Women's Sex-Role Attitudes, 1964–1974," *American Sociological Review* 41 (1976), pp. 573–596.

MAIN SOURCES OF SURVEY DATA

Gallup: Gallup data appear regularly in *The Gallup Report,* P.O. Box 628, Princeton, New Jersey 08542.

General Social Survey: See James Allen Davis and Tom W. Smith, *General Social Surveys, 1972–1988.* Chicago: National Opinion Research Center, 1988.

Monitoring the Future: See annual summary volumes by Jerald G. Bachman, Lloyd D. Johnston, and Patrick M. O'Malley. *Monitoring the Future: Questionnaire Responses from the Nation's High School Seniors.* Ann Arbor, Michigan: Institute for Social Research, University of Michigan.

3

RECENT CHANGES IN JAPANESE ATTITUDES

Sumiko Iwao

The norms and attitudes that shape Japanese life-styles and Japanese society as a whole have undergone significant change over the past decade. Indeed, a number of tendencies once cited as distinguishing characteristics of the Japanese people actually appear to have reversed themselves. Widespread generalizations about the Japanese among people in other countries, however, seem to remain more or less unchanged.

Although the focus of this essay on macro trends in attitudinal change may give the impression that Japanese society is changing uniformly and linearly, Japanese society, like any other human society, is actually composed of a wide variety of individuals, and, thus, the changes it is undergoing are much more complex than is widely believed. People's attitudes can differ according to the issue of focus, and their attitudes toward the same issue may differ according to their sex and age. Moreover, unlike Americans, who have low tolerance for inconsistencies in one's attitudes and one's behavior, Japanese tend to regard inconsistencies between opinions and behavior as something natural and inherent to social beings. It is not unusual, therefore, to witness mutually contradictory attitudinal changes simultaneously in Japanese society. For example, the Japanese do not find it particularly contradictory to simultaneously pursue "maintenance of the status quo" and diversity. In other words, the Japanese aspire to diversification and individualism as long as they do not affect their desire to stay happy. Indeed, it can be said that contemporary Japanese are seeking diversity *because* they are fully assured of the "maintenance of the status quo," that is, their happiness.[1]

FACTORS UNDERLYING ATTITUDINAL CHANGE

The speed of Japan's economic development, the accompanying level of affluence for relatively large segments of the general public, and the rapid shift to an aging society are the three most important factors underlying the value changes that divide the generations in Japan today. Until the mid-1970s, the Japanese people were caught up in the mechanisms of rapid economic growth and intent on achieving material satisfaction. The driving force with which they pursued these goals may be captured in such catchphrases as "Consumption is beautiful" and "The bigger, the better." The level of individual income was rising during this time, and many Japanese were rapidly reaching levels of material satisfaction they had once thought unattainable. Nonetheless, the expectation of future gratification shaped people's ways of thinking and living, and for that sake they were ready to forgo immediate satisfaction. This "rapid growth mentality" coincided with the era when Japan was intent on catching up with and surpassing the advanced nations of the West, and prevailed until it was gradually overtaken by the "slow growth mentality" that arose in the wake of the two oil crises.

Only after the majority of society had achieved a fairly high level of material well-being did Japanese begin to have the leisure to reflect on the quality of their lives, to turn their attention to nonmaterial fulfillment. The results of surveys on national life conducted annually by the Prime Minister's Office indicate that around 1978, the Japanese people began to attach more importance to spiritual fulfillment than to material affluence.[2] (This trend has continued, with those stressing material fulfillment dropping from 41 percent in 1977 to 34 percent in 1987, while those emphasizing spiritual fulfillment rose from 41 percent to 50 percent in the same period.) This trend is also observed in the results of the surveys on national character conducted by the Institute of Statistical Mathematics,[3] as indicated by responses to the following question: "In raising children of elementary school age, some people think that one should teach them that money is the most important thing in life. Do you agree with this statement or not?" The proportion of respondents agreeing has declined steadily since the mid-1950s,[4] reflecting an attitudinal shift toward a less positive evaluation of money and material things.

Within the context of these general shifts, we can isolate three major changes in Japanese character over the last decade: a tendency toward diversity and individuality, a need for swift results and instant gratification, and a desire for stability and maintenance of the status quo.

Diversity and Individuality

During the period when Japanese were still struggling to attain fundamental economic well-being, they lacked the confidence to make individual choices and decisions, and tended instead to tailor or adapt their behavior to that of people around them. As they became accustomed to affluence, however, they gradually gained the self-assurance to make choices and take action independently, rather than simply trying to "keep up with the Suzukis." The perception that most Japanese have nearly identical opinions about most things no longer is borne out by reality. Individual taste has become the major reference for choice, in place of duty, obligation, or conformity.

The Japanese seem to have gained confidence about themselves as a people. This can be observed in the changes in responses between 1953 and 1983 to the question, "In a word, are Japanese superior/equal/inferior to Westerners?" (see Figure 1, Annex Table A). The shift is remarkable in view of the fact that in 1953, more Japanese thought themselves to be inferior than superior. Both Japan's economic success and the rise in average level of education undoubtedly contributed to this trend.

The movement toward diversity and individuality in Japan is reflected in consumer behavior, as manufacturers are forced to switch from mass production of uniform goods to small-lot production of greater variety. One striking example is in the beer industry: the number of beer labels increased more than fivefold between 1975 and 1985, resulting in an average 76 percent cut in the output of each label. So, as beer production rose 21 percent

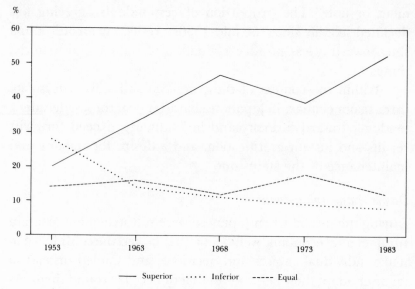

Source: Institute of Statistical Mathematics, *A Study of the Japanese National Character—The Seventh Nationwide Survey* (Tokyo, 1984).

Note: The data points are compiled in Table A in the Annex of this chapter.

FIG. 1.   DO YOU THINK THE JAPANESE ARE SUPERIOR, INFERIOR, OR EQUAL TO WESTERNERS?
(opinion polls of Japanese, percentage by year)

in the decade, Japanese consumers did not simply follow "fashionable" trends in picking their brew; rather, they displayed increasing selectivity in choosing between brands.

The same phenomenon can be seen across the spectrum of Japanese behavior and life-styles. A typical 35-year-old Japanese woman fifteen years ago, for example, was most likely a professional housewife with two children, who devoted her life to serving the needs of her husband and children. Today, she is equally likely to be single, married, living with a partner, or divorced; to have children or be childless; to be working part- or full-time; and to be a person who seeks fulfillment as an individual and devotes herself to personal goals. In other words, values, interests, and options have diversified, and people are experiencing the freedom to choose the kind of life-style they wish.

Instant Gratification

The traditional Japanese ethic of patience and perseverance appears to have given way to expectation of instant gratification of needs and desires. In the past, young people were taught that years of effort and hardship were required to reach some distant or difficult goal. The rapid spread of time-saving devices, such as microwave ovens and facsimile machines, along with the wide range of convenience services available today, has undermined such teachings. Now young people have come to expect and demand immediate returns for their efforts. Traditionally, people saved money a little at a time when they wanted to purchase something expensive, waiting until they had the entire amount necessary to buy it. Today, credit cards have eliminated the need for such patience and perseverance. Instant foods, stores open 24 hours a day, overnight delivery services, and the like mean people do not have to wait to get what they want.

In the workplace, people nowadays are less willing than they once were to put up with jobs they do not enjoy for the sake of promotion many years down the line. A survey by the Prime Minister's Office sought to determine the proportion of workers with an active, opportunity-seeking attitude toward changing jobs by asking: "Are you interested in seeking out and moving into a better job than your present one?" In 1983, 18 percent of men said yes and 77 percent said no.[5] As might be expected, the proportion giving affirmative replies was higher among men of younger age-groups, reaching 21 percent in the age 30–39 bracket and 30 percent of 20–29-year-olds. Only four years later 42 percent gave affirmative responses and 52 percent replied negatively to a similar question;[6] the affirmative responses were visibly more concentrated among better-educated groups (59 percent).

Even in 1983 the proportion willing to make a change was much higher than average among middle-management employees. An October 1983 poll of 1,000 such respondents (typically department or section chiefs in their mid-forties) by the leading economic daily, the *Nihon Keizai Shimbun,* asked "If another company came to you with a job offer, would you be prepared to accept it?" While 44 percent indicated that they would not, 55 percent answered that they would. These figures suggest that even six or seven years ago, the level of potential labor mobility was high. Today, workers are snapping up magazines specializing in job listings at a rate of 300,000 copies a week.

It should be pointed out here that when Japanese change jobs, it is usually not because of money or dissatisfaction with promotion opportunities. Under the current life-time employment/seniority system, the longer the tenure, the better the monetary and promotional compensation. Furthermore, Japanese tend to value job stability; they will not change to an unstable or risky job. Thus, when people shift employment it is more in order to find jobs they like, or to utilize their talents more fully. When Japanese hear of someone changing jobs, therefore, they usually do not interpret it in terms of money.

This impatience with achievement of goals is especially conspicuous among people born after around 1960. Unlike their parents, who grew up in less fortunate circumstances and in families with an average of about five children, these young people have been brought up amid considerable affluence in households with an average of 1.8 children. They have had little need to learn forbearance, are much more oriented toward immediate pleasures, and are much less motivated by the expectation of promotion in the workplace. We can say on the whole that Japanese are more relaxed than before and that they entertain hopes of leading life-styles of their own choosing (see Figure 2, Annex Table B).

The young people described above have come to be labeled by many as a "new breed." Their carefree attitude presents a special challenge to corporations, which until very recently have relied on the single-minded dedication of employees who put their work ahead of all else. The new breed—comprised of both men and women—rejects the one-dimensional values of older male employees, for whom work was—and remains—all-consuming. Younger workers aim instead for a balance of work and play. Even government authorities have finally begun to consider

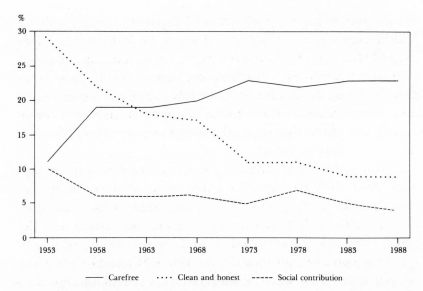

Source: Institute of Statistical Mathematics, *A Study of the Japanese National Character—The Eighth Nationwide Survey* (Tokyo, 1989).

Note: The data points are compiled in Table B in the Annex of this chapter.

FIG. 2.   WHAT KIND OF LIFE-STYLES DO YOU WISH TO ADOPT?
(opinion polls of Japanese, percentage by year)

the question of bringing Japanese working hours more into line with those of other countries.

Thus, although a trend in that direction is only getting under way, efforts to encourage people to spend less time at the office and more time in leisure activities have begun. The inescapable conclusion is that the legendary Japanese work ethic that facilitated the country's astounding economic growth is on the decline. This is a healthy change, even if it comes to mean a drop in productivity. Not surprisingly, however, the new attitudes sometimes raise the hackles of older men who devoted the better part of their lives to the good of their corporations during the era of rapid growth.

Stability and the Maintenance of the Status Quo

Various public opinion surveys indicate that the vast majority of Japanese today (75–90 percent, according to various polls) consider themselves members of the middle class. This by no means proves that so high a proportion of Japanese actually enjoy a middle-class way of life, however that may be defined, but it does suggest that a large majority *feel* they have achieved an "average" measure of prosperity. Furthermore, surveys show, most Japanese are basically satisfied with the way they live. Consequently, they are suspicious of any major changes in their lives, or in society as a whole, that might threaten the modest good fortune they have come to enjoy.

Despite their general satisfaction with their lives, many Japanese feel fairly strongly that some areas of their society are characterized by inequality and, indeed, unfairness. This is particularly true with regard to the current tax system and the reform legislation that passed in the Diet in 1988. According to the survey on social attitudes by the Prime Minister's Office, the proportion of those who considered the tax system unfair was 13 percent in 1980; this figure jumped to 41 percent in 1987.[7]

The traditional Japanese philosophy that "nothing is stable and nobody can enjoy prosperity forever," coupled with a growing perception of economic threat from the rapidly developing newly industrialized economies (the so-called NIEs), seems to have strengthened the desire on the part of many Japanese to maintain a safe status quo. They are all the more anxious to preserve their hard-won security now that the average life expectancy has risen to 75 years for men and 82 for women, necessitating serious preparations for a lengthy old age. The result is an impulse toward self-preservation and conservatism. Politically, this has taken the form of support for the ruling Liberal Democratic Party, even among young people, who used to be the flagbearers of radicalism and change.[8] When choosing jobs, though, as noted earlier, they may be open to change if they don't like their work, the young seem to place more importance on stability rather than growth potential, reflecting a disinclination to seek new challenges, and a great interest in settling down to a low-risk life.

FAMILY

Next, let us examine changes in attitudes toward family issues, particularly those that are relevant in the context of Japan–U.S.

relations. As the most basic unit of society, the family is both a mirror and an agent of social change and stability. Many people still imagine the typical Japanese family to be a close-knit, three-generation household, within which the elderly hold a respected and honored position. In actuality, however, the situation is quite different. The average Japanese household now has three members, and households consisting of only a married couple account for 21 percent of the total (up from 15 percent just a decade ago). Furthermore, 11 percent of Japanese are over 65 years old. This proportion is expected to climb to 16 percent by the turn of the century, and 24 percent by the year 2020. The majority of those who are over 65 and live alone are women. For this reason, women have shown greater interest than men in developments related to the formation of a gerontocratic society. The economic ramifications of the perceived need to prepare for old age include the prodigious growth of insurance packages and the entry of many married women into the labor market.

Interestingly enough, the concern about extended old age has affected Japanese attitudes toward children. Many people, particularly women, still view the process of raising their children as their most important mission in life, but the number of those believing that they should not "sacrifice their lives for their children" is increasing. Correspondingly, many desire to live in their old age independently of their married children if that is economically feasible. Such a desire brought out by changes in the parent-child relationship has contributed to a remarkable increase in women's participation in the labor force and to a growth in networking among them to help and support each other. Japanese parents—again, especially women—are, in this sense, slowly being weaned from their children. This will be necessary, too, considering that women are now likely to live until over the age of 80. The ideal popular among many older Japanese these days is living apart from their grown-up children, but close enough "to keep the soup hot." In a 1972 survey married women were asked what they considered the most desirable type of family: 42 percent chose the "child-centered family," whereas 25 percent selected the "husband-and-wife-centered family." Seven years later, however, the proportion of those answering "child-centered family" was down to 39 percent, while the proportion responding "husband-and-wife-centered family" rose to 30 percent.[9] Women's participation in the labor force has made it more difficult for women to be so-called "education mamas"—taking their children from one cram school to another. Consequently, women are investing less energy in their children's education, and instead more and more women are investing energy as well as money in their own activities and futures.

When thinking about any of the trends relating to the shape of the typical family, the overall decline in importance of the family itself should be taken into consideration. Japanese are increasingly thinking beyond the limits of their immediate families, because they know that they cannot depend upon their families as much as before. Whereas consideration for the well-being of one's own family outweighed the idea of serving society in the minds of most Japanese during the greater part of the 1970s and 1980s, the proportion of those desiring to be of service to society seems to be gradually increasing.

Along with the graying of society and the changing role of the Japanese family, another current concern among Japanese is "internationalization." While this catchword has come to encompass many of the issues facing Japan in its process of opening up to the rest of the world, it refers with particular emphasis to the problems revolving around foreigners living in Japan. Though the numbers of Japanese who have gone abroad and of foreigners residing in Japan have increased (see Table 1), and awareness of and support for foreign students in Japan has risen, the majority of Japanese remain insufficiently accepting of ethnic and racial differences. Social categorization of people as "insiders" or "outsiders" is still the norm. It might be pointed out that, for Japanese, this practice does not necessarily have a negative implication. Japanese who travel to the United States, for example, expect to be treated at arm's length, as visitors.

MARRIAGE

Attitudes toward marriage also have changed (see Table 2). Fewer people hold the naive view that "happiness lies in mar-

TABLE 1. FOREIGN TRAVELERS TO JAPAN, JAPANESE OVERSEAS
TRAVELERS, NUMBER OF INTERNATIONAL MARRIAGES
AND NUMBER OF FOREIGN STUDENTS IN JAPAN *(by year)*

Year	Foreign travelers to Japan	Japanese overseas travelers	Foreign residents in Japan*	# of marriages in Japan	Int'l marriages in Japan	Foreign students in Japan
1965	291,309	265,683	665,989	954,852	4,156	NA
1970	775,061	608,379	708,458	1,029,405	5,546	NA
1975	780,298	2,446,236	751,842	941,628	6,045	5,573
1980	1,295,866	3,909,333	782,910	774,702	7,261	6,572
1985	2,259,894	4,948,366	850,612	723,669	12,181	15,009
1986	2,021,450	5,516,193	867,237	698,431	12,529	18,631
1987	2,161,275	6,829,338	941,005	681,589	14,584	22,154

Source: Ministry of Justice, Judicial System and Research Department, *Annual Report of Statistics on Legal Migrants* (Tokyo, various years).

* Number of holders of "alien registration card"
NA = not available

TABLE 2. JAPANESE ATTITUDES TOWARD MARRIAGE
(opinion polls of Japanese, percentage by year)

Attitude	1979	1984	1987		
			Total	Male	Female
It is better to marry	73.8%	72.4%	73.6%	78.7%	69.8%
It is not necessary to marry	18.9	20.3	20.8	15.7	24.7
Don't know	7.3	7.3	5.5	5.6	5.5
Total	*100.0*	*100.0*	*100.0*	*100.0*	*100.0*

Source: Prime Minister's Office, *Opinion Survey on Social Attitudes* (Tokyo, 1989).

Note: Figures do not add exactly because of rounding.

riage," and an increasing proportion—roughly 25 percent of women—feel that if they can get by economically alone, there is no need to marry. Women's growing economic independence, a general tolerance of relationships between unmarried men and women, and a variety of other factors have led to an increase in the number of men and women who delay marriage or even decide not to marry at all. Nonetheless, sooner or later, most people desire to and do get married. Still, some men are experiencing greater difficulty in finding spouses and, in particular, men in rural areas are often unable to find Japanese women willing to lead that kind of hard and relatively isolated life and are marrying non-Japanese, particularly Filipinas and Koreans.

DIVORCE

As might be expected, attitudes toward divorce are also in transition. Various surveys reveal that over 60 percent of adults feel that "in some circumstances" divorce is "permissible." Among women in their twenties, 72 percent profess a tolerant view of divorce, while only 25 percent have a negative attitude toward it. Nonetheless, Japan's divorce rate remains considerably lower than that of other advanced industrial countries. In 1983, the divorce rate per 1,000 population was 1.5 in Japan, compared with 5.0 in the United States. Perhaps more enlightening, however, are the statistics on divorce by duration of marriage. From 1970 to 1983, the proportion of all divorces occurring in the first five years of marriage dropped from 52 percent to 32 percent while the proportion among couples who had been married for ten years or more rose from 24 percent to 45 percent.

Whereas once women most commonly cited their husband's brutality or unfaithfulness as grounds for divorce, now the reasons tend to be more abstract, such as lack of an emotional bond. Thus, the traditional notion that, in an ideal marriage, "husband and wife are like the air"—meaning that they need each other for survival, though they may not actually feel each other's existence—apparently is giving way to the Western ideal of a couple's actively relating to each other as individuals. It seems, however, many more women than men have shifted to this viewpoint.

Traditionally, the husband served as a sort of diplomat for the family, acting as official communicator with the world outside the home. He was the "gatekeeper" of information flowing in and out of the home, and thus maintained his high status within the family unit. Women were responsible only for domestic affairs. I once met a woman in her late thirties who had entered university when her children were old enough to require less attention. Sitting for an examination on one occasion, she mistakenly wrote her husband's name on her examination paper instead of her own, because she had always signed her husband's name on important documents. This is symbolic of the difficulty women face in making the transition from wife to individual in Japan.

FEMALE ROLES

One factor frequently cited in discussions of divorce is the changing role of women in Japanese society. For many years, both the stability of the family and the productivity of the workplace— and, by extension, the nation's economic growth—have been supported by a strong foundation of self-sacrificing women. For the most part, women have been content with vicarious fulfillment through the achievements of husbands and children, who have been free to devote their full energies to work and school, respectively, thanks to their wives' and mothers' attentive support. But rising education levels, along with the dissemination of time-saving household appliances and the decreasing size of the family, have begun to make it possible for women to seek fulfillment outside the home. Also, it is only natural that a woman's outlook on life tends to change when she knows she will have 30 years of life left to her after her youngest child has reached adulthood.

Not long ago, the female work force consisted basically of young single women who intended to work until they married. Those who continued working after marriage were generally thought to be doing so because their husbands were undependable. Today, approximately half of all married women hold full- or part-time jobs. The most common pattern among women is to quit work when they marry or get pregnant, devote themselves to housework and child rearing for seven or eight years, and then return to the work force about the time the youngest child has started school. An increasing number of both women and men seem to support this practice (see Table 3). It is notable that not only women but men have changed their attitudes toward women's work. According to a survey compiled by the government's Management and Coordination Agency in 1987, among mothers joining the labor force, economic considerations top the list of reasons given for working (38 percent). This is followed by "to fill free time" (11 percent) and "to make use of skills and abilities" (5 percent). These figures have remained fairly constant since 1980.[10]

Communication between husband and wife in Japan is generally not very extensive, as the husband is expected to work

TABLE 3. JAPANESE MEN AND WOMEN AGREEING WITH VARIOUS
STATEMENTS REGARDING WOMEN'S CAREER PURSUITS
(*opinion polls of Japanese, percentage by year*)

Statement	1972		1984	
	Male	*Female*	*Male*	*Female*
Women should not work at all	7.8%	15.9%	6.1%	9.8%
Women should work until marriage	18.6	26.2	11.1	16.4
Women should work until child-birth	12.3	15.6	10.6	13.4
Women should continue working even after childbirth	11.5	9.7	20.1	15.7
Women should quit their jobs upon childbirth, but should work again when their children are old enough	39.5	20.9	45.3	36.1
Don't know	10.3	11.5	6.9	8.6
Total	*100.0*	*100.0*	*100.0*	*100.0*

Source: Institute of Statistical Mathematics, *A Study of the Japanese National Character—The Eighth Nationwide Survey* (Tokyo, 1989).

Note: Figures do not add exactly because of rounding.

long hours. As the number of women receiving higher education and working as professionals outside the home has risen and as the flood of information reaching women directly at home through the mass media has increased, women have ceased depending entirely on their husbands' decisions and have grown more independent. They now make important decisions by themselves without the input of their often workaholic spouses. Furthermore, women seem to be enjoying their lives more than before, as is indicated in the responses obtained to the survey question, "If you were reborn, would you choose to be reborn as a man or a woman?" (see Figure 3, Annex Table C).

MALE ROLES

In Japan, as in many countries, the husband has traditionally taken pride in being the sole breadwinner and in his family's

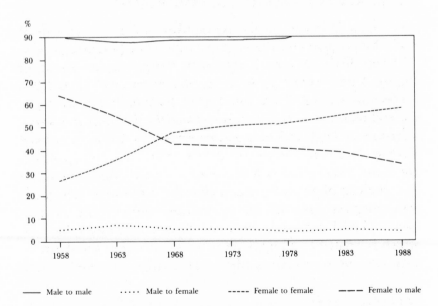

Source: Institute of Statistical Mathematics, *A Study of the Japanese National Character—The Eighth Nationwide Survey* (Tokyo, 1989).

Note: The data points are compiled in Table C in the Annex of this chapter.

FIG. 3.   DO YOU WISH TO BE REBORN AS A MAN OR WOMAN?
(opinion polls of Japanese, percentage by year)

complete dependence upon him. Once, the typical pattern was for the husband to bring home his pay in a cash envelope. Reinforcing the children's sense of the father's authority and role as breadwinner, he would hand it unopened to his wife, who would receive it with a sincere bow and words of gratitude as the children looked on in awe at an important family ritual. These days, by contrast, wages are most often transferred directly to employees' bank accounts through a computer network, and the wife draws upon and spends them as she sees fit to cover family expenses. The husband even receives his pocket money from her. Many children today therefore do not have a clear idea that it is the father who is actually earning most or all of the family income, and this gives them the impression that the mother holds greater power. Thus, the balance of power in the home apparently has shifted from husband to wife.

EVALUATION OF SOCIETAL CONDITIONS

The Prime Minister's Office has studied public perceptions of both the positive and the negative aspects of Japanese society. The top three of each, as chosen by the public, are shown in Figure 4 and Annex Table D. Each year from 1984 to 1988, "economic strength" was cited most frequently among those societal features seen as positive; dissatisfaction over the severe shortage of land and housing, especially in Tokyo, increased sharply after 1985 and topped the list of negative perceptions in the most recent surveys. Despite some annual fluctuations, on the whole, a higher proportion view the direction of the country's progress positively than negatively—40 percent, as compared with 31 percent in 1987 (see Figure 5, Annex Table E)—which is related to a high level of satisfaction and the desire to maintain the status quo, rather than change, as stated earlier.

NATIONALISM

Nationalism can be conceived of in different ways and on different levels, so the following results of a survey conducted by the Prime Minister's Office on the strength of positive feelings toward the country should be treated cautiously. Not much change

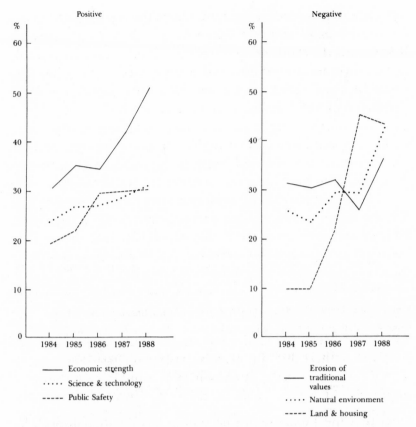

Positive

Negative

Source: Prime Minister's Office, *Opinion Survey on Social Attitudes* (Tokyo, 1989).

Note: The data points are compiled in Table D in the Annex of this chapter.

FIG. 4.   FEATURES OF JAPANESE SOCIETY MOST COMMONLY
PERCEIVED AS POSITIVE AND NEGATIVE
(opinion polls of Japanese, percentage by year)

can be observed in the degree of patriotism during the last ten years or so. One notable point, however, is that those who have lived abroad express a markedly stronger love of country than average Japanese (see Figure 6, Annex Table F). As more and more Japanese spend part of their lives abroad the proportion expressing a strong love of country is likely to increase.

The larger proportion of people evaluating Japanese as superior to Westerners, which was noted earlier, might also be interpreted as a sign of increasing nationalism. Still, it does not

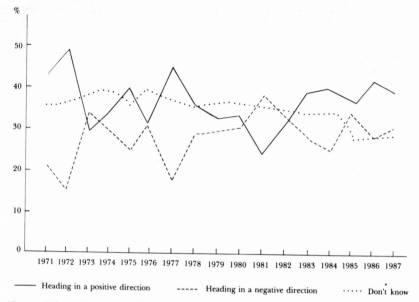

────── Heading in a positive direction   ----- Heading in a negative direction   ····· Don't know

Source: Prime Minister's Office, *Opinion Survey on Social Attitudes* (Tokyo, 1989).

Note: The data points are compiled in Table E in the Annex of this chapter.

FIG. 5.   PERCEPTIONS OF JAPANESE REGARDING DIRECTION
OF COUNTRY'S PROGRESS
(opinion polls of Japanese, percentage by year)

seem that the Japanese are becoming more nationalistic. The 1987 survey on diplomacy conducted by the Prime Minister's Office indicates that the proportion of people in favor of accepting more foreign workers (laborers) is larger than the proportion against it (31 percent, as compared with 18 percent).[11]

ATTITUDES TOWARD THE UNITED STATES

The proportion of those expressing affinity toward the United States (again, according to the Prime Minister's Office) has stayed more or less stable since 1978. Although it decreased 8 points between 1985 and 1986, it recovered more than 4 points in 1987 (see Table 4). It is notable that a higher proportion of men than of women feel affinity toward the United States (80 percent versus 68 percent) and the proportion among those in their forties (78 percent) is the highest among different age groups.

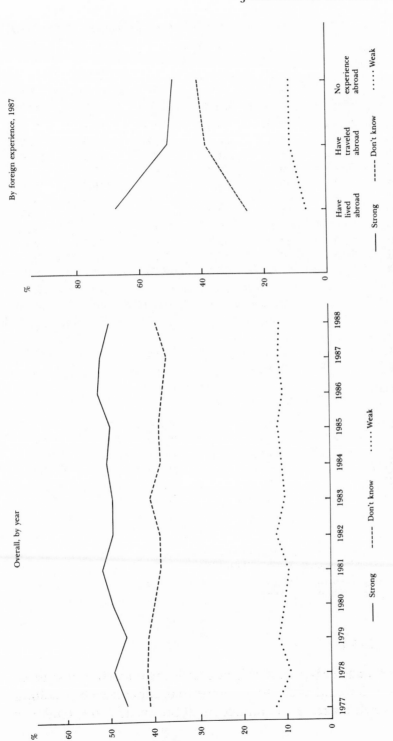

By foreign experience, 1987

Overall, by year

Source: Prime Minister's Office, *Opinion Survey on Social Attitudes* (Tokyo, 1989).

Note: The data points are compiled in Table F in the Annex of this chapter.

FIG. 6. PATRIOTISM IN JAPAN

TABLE 4. AFFINITY FOR THE UNITED STATES *(opinion polls of Japanese)*

Overall, by year

		Positive			Negative	
	Total	Much affinity	Some affinity	Total	Not very much	No affinity
1978	72.7%	33.4%	39.3%	19.4%	11.5%	7.9%
1979	78.0	39.3	38.7	16.8	10.9	5.9
1980	77.2	38.3	38.9	17.7	12.2	5.5
1981	69.4	29.1	40.3	24.7	17.8	6.9
1982	71.4	30.4	41.0	23.6	16.7	6.9
1983	71.9	28.2	43.7	22.6	16.5	6.1
1984	74.9	34.0	40.9	21.5	15.5	6.0
1985	75.6	36.2	39.4	19.7	15.5	4.2
1986	67.5	27.7	39.8	27.5	20.4	7.1
1987	72.2	30.1	42.1	23.1	15.3	7.8
1988	73.6	33.4	40.2	21.5	14.7	6.8

By sex and age group, October 1988

	Yes*	No**	Don't know
Average	73.6%	21.5%	4.8%
Male	79.6	17.4	2.9
Female	67.8	25.6	6.7
Age Group			
20–29	72.8	24.8	2.4
30–39	73.6	22.7	3.7
40–49	78.2	18.9	2.8
50–59	73.9	21.1	5.0
60–69	70.6	21.7	7.8
70–	67.9	21.6	10.5

Source: Institute of Statistical Mathematics, *A Study of the Japanese National Character—The Eighth Nationwide Survey* (Tokyo, 1989).

* yes = very much and a little
** no = not a bit and not particularly

SUMMARY

The change in Japanese attitudes, growing out of a firm sense of satisfaction and with the advent of an aging society resulting from affluence, is manifested in three trends: the tendency toward diversity and individuality, the demand for swift results and instant gratification, and the desire for stability and maintenance of the status quo. As a result, the view of work is steadily shifting away from the old apprenticeship mold and toward the perspective that work is a humane, enjoyable part of life. Meanwhile, greater heterogeneity in life-styles and values is replacing the traditional uniformity and homogeneity. The implications of these changes are positive in the sense that they may make Japan more open to relations with other countries, the United States included.

It should also be pointed out that the elements of change, including the shift of focus within the family from the traditional parent-child relationship to that between the married couple, the increase in the number of working wives, and the increase in the number of offices closed on Saturdays, will eventually shift the orientation of Japanese values from work to the family. This tendency is particularly notable among the younger generation, and, as the cost for a more humane life-style, may eventually adversely affect Japan's productivity (though not the quality of Japanese products), mitigating the severity of the competition between the United States and Japan.

At the same time, the Japanese reveal a strong sense of satisfaction with the level of affluence they now enjoy, and of determination to see that the status quo is not disturbed. They firmly resist external pressures, such as those from the United States, that demand change in the status quo.

Although Japanese views of the United States continue to be positive, we cannot overlook a tendency on the part of Japanese to feel less affinity toward Americans when they feel strongly pressured by the United States. Japanese are gaining greater confidence as a people, and this adds all the more to their disillusionment with the United States over bilateral conflicts. The potential danger is that overconfidence among Japanese can lead them to arrogant behavior, which could have a negative impact on American attitudes toward Japan.

Major changes are taking place in the Japanese family and in views of the family, but there is nothing to indicate that the changes might threaten the stability of society.

Regarding racial prejudice among Japanese, no marked change is visible, but a strong reaction is possible should the United States and Japan seriously clash over some issue (such as hiring practices of Japanese companies located in the United States). In quantitative terms, the internationalization of Japanese society is progressing; qualitatively, however, the genuine internationalization of Japanese thinking is an issue yet to be fully confronted.

Japan and the United States must work together, seeking solutions to the problems they face by learning from each other. Among specific problems are the aging of society and educational reform.

ANNEX

TABLE A.   DO YOU THINK THE JAPANESE ARE SUPERIOR, INFERIOR, OR EQUAL TO WESTERNERS?
(opinion polls of Japanese, percentage by year)

	1953	1963	1968	1973	1983
Superior	20.0%	33.0%	47.0%	39.0%	53.0%
Inferior	28.0	14.0	11.0	9.0	8.0
Equal	14.0	16.0	12.0	18.0	12.0

Source: Institute of Statistical Mathematics, *A Study of the Japanese National Character—The Seventh Nationwide Survey* (Tokyo, 1984).

Note: These data are also presented in Figure 1.

TABLE B.   WHAT KIND OF LIFE-STYLE DO YOU WISH TO ADOPT?
(opinion polls of Japanese, percentage by year)

	1953	1958	1963	1968	1973	1978	1983	1988
To live carefree	11%	19%	19%	20%	23%	22%	23%	23%
To live cleanly & honestly	29	22	18	17	11	11	9	9
To contribute to society	10	6	6	6	5	7	5	4

Source: Institute of Statistical Mathematics, *A Study of the Japanese National Character—The Eighth Nationwide Survey* (Tokyo, 1989).

Note: These data are also presented in Figure 2.

TABLE C.   WOULD YOU CHOOSE TO BE REBORN AS A MAN OR WOMAN?
(opinion polls of Japanese, percentage by year)

	1958	1963	1968	1973	1978	1983	1988
Male to male	90%	88%	89%	89%	90%	90%	90%
Male to female	5	7	5	5	4	5	4
Female to female	27	36	48	51	52	56	59
Female to male	64	55	43	42	41	39	34

Source: Institute of Statistical Mathematics, *A Study of the Japanese National Character—The Eighth Nationwide Survey* (Tokyo, 1989).

Note: These data are also presented in Figure 3.

TABLE D. FEATURES OF JAPANESE SOCIETY MOST COMMONLY
PERCEIVED AS POSITIVE AND NEGATIVE
(opinion polls of Japanese, percentage by year)

	Positive				
	1984	*1985*	*1986*	*1987*	*1988*
Economic strength	30.4%	35.0%	34.2%	41.5%	50.6%
Science & technology	23.6	26.5	26.8	28.5	30.7
Public safety	19.3	21.7	29.1	29.7	30.0
	Negative				
	1984	*1985*	*1986*	*1987*	*1988*
Erosion of traditional values	31.4%	30.1%	32.0%	26.0%	36.3%
Natural environment	25.4	23.3	29.5	29.4	42.9
Land & housing	9.9	9.6	21.9	45.1	43.5

Source: Prime Minister's Office, *Opinion Survey on Social Attitudes* (Tokyo, 1989).

Note: These data are also presented in Figure 4.

TABLE E. PERCEPTIONS OF JAPANESE REGARDING DIRECTION OF
COUNTRY'S PROGRESS
(opinion polls of Japanese, percentage by year)

	1971	*1975*	*1979*	*1983*	*1987*
Heading in a positive direction	43.3%	39.5%	33.1%	39.3%	39.6%
Heading in a negative direction	21.1	25.2	30.3	26.8	31.4
Don't know	35.6	35.3	36.6	33.9	29.0

Source: Prime Minister's Office, *Opinion Survey on Social Attitudes* (Tokyo, 1989).

Note: These data are also presented in Figure 5.

TABLE F.   PATRIOTISM IN JAPAN

Overall, by year

	1977	*1981*	*1985*	*1988*
Strong	46.2%	51.9%	49.6%	49.6%
Weak	12.5	9.5	11.7	11.1
Don't know	41.3	38.7	38.7	39.4

By foreign experience, 1987

	Have lived abroad	*Have traveled abroad*	*No experience abroad*
Strong	67.7%	50.5%	48.4%
Weak	6.5	11.1	11.3
Don't know	25.8	38.4	40.3

Source: Prime Minister's Office, *Opinion Survey on Social Attitudes* (Tokyo, 1989).

Note: These data are also presented in Figure 6.

NOTES

1. American readers should keep in mind that application of American values to measure Japanese behavior will lead to misinterpretation and misunderstanding. Needless to say, the same rule applies to Japanese measuring American behavior. This warning is particularly relevant in this essay because space limitations do not allow the author to explain the complex background of each attitude discussed.
2. Prime Minister's Office, *Opinion Survey on National Life* (Tokyo, various years).
3. Institute of Statistical Mathematics, *A Study of the Japanese National Character* (Tokyo, 1954, 1974, 1984). The Institute is an affiliate organization of the Ministry of Education, Science and Culture.
4. Agreement was 65 percent and disagreement was 24 percent in 1953; 44 percent and 38 percent, respectively, in 1973; and 43 percent and 42 percent, respectively, in 1983. Institute of Statistical Mathematics, *A Study of the Japanese National Character—The Seventh Nationwide Survey* (Tokyo, 1984).
5. Prime Minister's Office, *Opinion Survey on Work and Life* (Tokyo, 1984).
6. "If you could apply your abilities, would you be willing to change jobs?"
7. Prime Minister's Office, *Opinion Survey on Social Attitudes* (Tokyo, 1981 and 1988).
8. The House of Councilors election in July 1989 was unique because the major issue (consumption tax) was unusually salient. Housewives played

an active role, which contributed to the Socialist victory. However, many younger voters did not cast votes and stayed politically indifferent.

9. Prime Minister's Office, *Opinion Survey on Family and Household* (Tokyo, 1973 and 1980).

10. Management and Coordination Agency, *Basic Survey on Employment Structure* (Tokyo, 1987).

11. Prime Minister's Office, *Opinion Survey on Foreign Policy* (Tokyo, 1989).

4

U.S. INDUSTRIAL CULTURE AND THE JAPANESE COMPETITIVE CHALLENGE

D. Eleanor Westney

One of the most striking aspects of U.S. industrial culture today is the extent to which any discussion of current issues involves Japan. The single most important influence on U.S. industry over the last decade has been Japanese competition, which has moved from such basic industries as steel and automobiles into sectors that have long been regarded as bastions of American dominance, including semiconductors, supercomputers, and telecommunications equipment. The consequence is what the founder of the Boston Consulting Group has called "the ongoing manufacturing revolution triggered by Japanese innovation."[1] Japanese competition has confronted U.S. industry with fundamental challenges to its institutions, its industrial technologies, and its most cherished assumptions about management.

Over the last decade the statements of managers and the business press in the United States have focused on four major arenas in which U.S. industry must improve its competitiveness: quality, productivity, product development (the rapid development and manufacture of goods that appeal to users in the United States and worldwide), and price competition. The first three are primarily management variables; the fourth has been the ground of most of the trade tensions and public policy debates of the last decade. Japanese firms are seen as having unfair advantages over their U.S. counterparts in price competition because of an array of institutional factors that cannot be addressed at the level of the firm.

The dual challenge of Japanese competition—to industrial management and the industrial system in the United States—and the emerging U.S. response are the themes of the following discussion.

THE JAPANESE CHALLENGE TO U.S. INDUSTRIAL MANAGEMENT

In a number of industries where "best practice" was for decades defined by U.S. firms, Japanese companies have managed to set new standards for quality, productivity, and—despite the much-criticized insularity of the Japanese—developing products that meet the needs of users worldwide. The obvious question for the last decade has been: How? A somewhat suspect characteristic of the large body of literature trying to answer this question has been the eagerness of many management experts to locate the key to Japan's success in greater reverence in Japan for their own particular area of expertise. Production and operations experts have published articles with titles like "Japan—Where Operations Really Are Strategic";[2] marketing professors have extolled Japanese marketing strategies;[3] human resources specialists have found the key to success in Japanese personnel development programs.[4]

The portrayals of Japanese management that have reached U.S. managers have therefore been filtered through the perceptions of U.S. management experts who have seen embodied in the best of the Japanese system the principles and practices that they themselves have long espoused, and they have so translated them to their Western audiences. Often they have ignored or downplayed elements that are less congenial to their own predispositions or to U.S. management culture—such as linking top corporate salary increases to the scale of the increments won by blue collar workers, or the low rewards and lack of security of the "temporary employees" who provide an expendable workforce that cushions the firm's permanent employees. Not surprisingly, critics have responded with a growing literature focused on the less impressive aspects of Japanese industrial management, such as discriminatory treatment of women and older workers, the lower level of protection for consumers against collusive business practices, and the heavy demands that many companies place on the time and the emotional loyalties of their managers.[5] The glowing descriptions of the Japanese production system have been increasingly shouldered aside by reports that efforts to adopt specific "keys" to Japanese manufacturing success, such as quality control circles and just-in-time logistics systems, have been meeting with mixed results in U.S. companies.[6]

The growing literature debunking the Japanese model for success has warned that Japan is not an appropriate model for the United States and that the wrong factors have been identified as key elements of the model. But even the most ardent advocates of these positions have not denied that the Japanese challenge has demanded changes in industrial management in the United States, if not by learning from Japanese models, then by developing distinctive patterns that can serve as functional equivalents. The reassessment of U.S. industrial management practices has focused on four major areas:

Utilizing and enhancing worker know-how. Underlying Japan's quality control circles, suggestion systems, *kaizen* (continuous improvement) programs, and "zero defects" movement is management's recognition that the problems and prospects for improvement in any job are best understood by the people doing the job. This requires organizational systems that provide incentives for workers to think of ways to improve production processes and that equip them as much as possible with the means to carry out those improvements. Such systems are based on a number of assumptions that are often implicit rather than explicit: (a) process improvement is a dynamic and continuous undertaking, not a stage on the way to a stable state where, once again, the emphasis will be on maintenance and control rather than improvement and change; (b) the improvement of quality and productivity is recognized by both management and workers as the major criterion for assessing proposed changes in workplace systems; (c) the benefits of improvement will be shared (for example, improved productivity will not result in a reduction of the workforce). The involvement of production workers in process improvements appears to be especially important in flexible manufacturing systems, where worker involvement in extending the capacities of the equipment is increasingly recognized as critical in realizing the full benefits of the technology.[7]

Linkages across functions. The ways in which the most successful Japanese firms move people between product development and production is a key element of their approach to quality ("designing for manufacturability") and of the speed with which new products are brought to market. The higher level of specialization of training and careers that has prevailed in most U.S. firms may have produced greater levels of expertise within each function, but it has tended to be a handicap in communicating across functions. Japanese firms have also tended to organize their research and development (R&D) functions so that a significant part of their resources, both financial and human, is committed to continuous incremental innovation in manufacturing processes and in products. Consumer electronics provides the most widely recognized example of a continuous stream of new models in a given product line, with only moderate change in their basic design.

Utilizing and enhancing supplier know-how. The relationships between Japan's large manufacturing firms and their suppliers is another management factor seen as contributing to enhanced quality and productivity. Whereas the dominant U.S. system traditionally has been based on arm's-length relationships determined primarily by price and by mutual desires to minimize interdependence, the Japanese system has relied on close multiple linkages between corporations and their suppliers. The typical large Japanese firm relies on outside suppliers for more of its components than does its U.S. counterpart, but it uses a much smaller number of suppliers for each component. These suppliers are linked to the firm by shared quality control systems and R&D resources (both financial and human). The system ties the production processes of suppliers closely to its own through just-in-time delivery systems, and relies more on performance specifications than on design specifications, "to let the supplier innovate—after all, the supplier is the expert."[8]

Close customer contacts. The capacity to develop products that appeal to users in foreign as well as domestic markets is another arena where Japanese competition has often forced U.S. firms to reexamine their management practices, especially their strong reliance on quantitative marketing research and marketing models. Japanese companies, most notably those in consumer products, have focused instead on understanding user needs in context, through intense contacts with customers, the continuous monitoring of distribution channels, and careful analysis of competitors' products. They have shown a remarkable ability to do this on a global basis, although it is worth noting that their success has been greatest in industries where the demands of the Japanese market and those of foreign markets are quite similar (they have been less successful to date in such industries as pharmaceuticals and packaged food products, where the Japanese market differs substantially from other major markets).

Underlying these four aspects of management is an orientation to continuous innovation, to what can be called the "Red Queen" syndrome of running strenuously even to stay in the same place in a dynamic industrial system. In the intense competitiveness and the rapid changes of the postwar Japanese business environment, it has been extremely difficult to keep competitors from emulating or trying to outdo any innovations in products, processes, or management systems. In many industries in the Japanese business environment, as one Japanese manager has explained, "if something works, within six months everyone is doing it."[9] Given the difficulties of maintaining a monopoly on any particular innovation, the innovation itself has been less important than the capacity to generate further innovations. This presents something of a contrast to the orientation of U.S. managers and management theorists, who until recently have tended to see innovation or change as a transition between stable states, and to emphasize capturing the benefits of innovation through secrecy or through intellectual property laws.

In addition, Japanese management systems have focused attention on the importance in a dynamic environment of "learning networks" (linkages within the firm and across its boundaries that increase its knowledge base), and do so not only by bringing knowledge across the boundaries so that value can be added to it internally but also by generating knowledge jointly with other organizations. The most important networks include suppliers and customers, although those networks involving joint research with competitors under government sponsorship have received more attention from Western management analysts. In some ways, therefore, although the United States has long been portrayed as the first "information-intensive society," Japan can be seen as the leader in the development of "information-intensive manufacturing." As a result, Japan has come to pose a major challenge to U.S. industrial management.

THE RESPONSE OF U.S. INDUSTRY

The last decade has witnessed a continuing debate over what, if anything, U.S. industrial management can learn from Japan. Two diametrically opposed positions have dominated discussions. One is that since good industrial and management practice is universal, Japanese best practice provides not only a challenge but also a model for U.S. managers.[10] The other is that since good industrial and management practice is deeply rooted in a society's culture and institutions, Japanese practices cannot and should not be models for Western organizations. The first position assumes that there are virtually no limits on learning from Japan, except perhaps a reluctance to learn; the second, that there is virtually nothing to learn.

But even as the debate goes on, what was once primarily a one-way flow of learning across cultures—Japanese managers learning from the United States—has become a two-way flow. Growing numbers of U.S. managers are traveling to Japan on assessment and study missions comparable to those that the Japanese have made to the United States for years: visiting factories and laboratories, interviewing managers of top firms, listening to presentations by local management experts. The number of linkages between U.S. and Japanese firms in which the U.S. firm seeks either technology or know-how from its Japanese partner is steadily increasing. U.S. firms are intensifying their efforts to penetrate the Japanese marketplace, both to challenge their Japanese competitors on their home ground and to gain knowledge to apply in their worldwide operations.

In the process, it has become clear that the constraints on learning are not limited to a reluctance to learn. Some fundamental assumptions of U.S. industrial management are very different from those undergirding the Japanese systems. Perhaps the most widely noted (and most widely criticized, in the light of recent "merger mania") is the U.S. management view of the corporation as a bundle of financial assets. The oft-voiced credo of U.S. managers that their primary obligation is generating value for the shareholders is built on the assumption that the most important resources of the firm are financial. The knowledge and learning capacity provided by the firm's employees take second place, perhaps because of the ideological commitment to the concept of efficient markets in which financial resources enable one to buy all other resources. Where a Japanese firm may well choose to foster a new set of technologies and products in order to enhance its technological capacities, its U.S. counterpart will often rely on a sophisticated analysis of the costs and expected returns on the investment.

A second fundamental feature of U.S. industrial management is the strong commitment to managerial autonomy. U.S. managers have long been hostile to any interventions in the firm—by unions, the state, or financial institutions—or to any ties with outside organizations that might lead to an erosion of the company's proprietary technology and independence. This desire for autonomy has, of course, been strongly reinforced by U.S. antitrust law, which is relatively quick to define cooperation between firms as collusion. A third and long-standing characteristic of U.S. management is its technocratic bias, with its emphasis on equipping managers with the expertise and the analytical tools to solve problems, rather than to organize problem solving, and its corresponding tendency to look for technological solutions. Finally, as noted above, U.S. corporate strategy has long been oriented to capturing the benefits of innovation and to niche strategies (through which a firm can earn high profits by developing distinctive products or services that competitors find difficult to match).

Despite the strength of these attitudinal factors, they have been less potent barriers to change than critics in the early 1980s expected. The process by which Japanese best practice was filtered through the perceptions and the language of U.S. management experts made it at least partly compatible with existing assumptions. And in several industries Japanese competition was a challenge serious enough to force a recognition that change could not wait for a revolution in managerial thinking.

Attitudinal factors are not, of course, the only constraints on learning from Japan. The differences between the two societies in labor markets and labor organization, capital markets, legal systems, and even geography mean that the U.S. response to the Japanese challenge has been a process of adapting some of the most visible Japanese innovations in manufacturing organization to the very different U.S. environment, as well as trying to develop distinctively U.S. alternatives.

Perhaps the most dramatic changes over the last decade have occurred in the U.S. industrial relations system, with the shift away from the collective bargaining system institutionalized in the 1930s. Experts have seen this shift as a necessary condition for developing systems to involve production workers in quality and productivity improvement.[11] The New Deal system was centered on collective bargaining over wages, hours, and working conditions (in terms of worker safety and comfort); pattern bargaining, which set common standards within and often across industries; job control unionism, which demanded highly formalized contracts specifying wages for each job and ensuring the allocation of jobs by seniority; and quasi-judicial grievance procedures, in which the union acted as worker advocate. The system was grounded on the assumption of a fundamental but manageable conflict of interest between management and labor. It therefore turned to a political model, which institutionalized worker rights to representation through unions and union rights in the bargaining process. The state assumed the tasks of monitoring and enforcing those rights.

U.S. managers never fully embraced the New Deal system, and throughout the postwar period, they adopted union avoidance strategies wherever possible (by locating new plants in regions where unions were weak, for example). The impact was muted as long as one of the major union avoidance tactics was to anticipate worker demands by introducing into nonunion plants the principal aspects of the New Deal system: following the wage and working conditions settlements reached in collective bargaining elsewhere, for example, and adopting job categories, seniority systems, and grievance procedures modeled on those of union plants. Management's aversion to unions became a major force for change only when the pressure of Japanese competition in autos and steel, two of the leading sectors in the New Deal system, led to the development of an alternative model in the late 1970s and early 1980s.

The new model, which a recent analysis has dubbed the "non-union human resource management system,"[12] rejected the centralized collective bargaining process in favor of a wide variety of management-labor interactions at the level of the firm and of compensation systems that were contingent on productivity gains, quality improvement, and overall firm performance. It also rejected a job-focused system in favor of one much more akin to the management bureaucracies, in which pay is based on education or training (rather than on the specific job being performed), flexible job categories and work assignments, and team organization. The new system incorporated to some extent the older insistence on due process for worker grievances, but supplemented such structures with a variety of informal and formal communication mechanisms, such as the "open door" policy of supervisors, suggestions systems, ombudsmen, management-labor meetings, and "management by walking around." These alternatives are based on the assumption that conflicts within the firm are due to personality clashes or faulty communication rather than to fundamental conflicts of interest. By the mid-1980s, plants that had institutionalized the new systems replaced union plants as the recognized centers of innovation in work organization and industrial relations. Concession bargaining in the face of the eroding competitive position of major U.S. firms has not only forced unions to give back past gains on wages and hours but has also institutionalized the new system as a model for worker organization and for the bargaining process itself, which has shifted its focus from the industry to the individual firm.

The new system was a major change in the U.S. industrial system, but it was less revolutionary than it may have appeared. It was solidly premised on human relations theories of motivation that had first been articulated in the United States in the 1920s and 1930s. In the mid-1950s, Reinhard Bendix noted in his classic study of U.S. management ideology that "there are indications that many American managers have adopted the *language* of the human relations approach, whether or not they have adopted the practices or its ideas."[13] The new industrial relations system can be viewed as extending the techniques of managing human resources that have been developed for managerial personnel further down the organization, onto the factory floor. In addition, the new model's rejection of industrial and craft unions and of the role of the state as mediator and umpire in a tripartite industrial relations system fits the long-standing U.S. managerial prejudices against outside interference in the management of the firm.

The same legitimating framework of the human relations school has also helped in the introduction of changes in the organization of product development. These changes have drawn much less attention in the general press, but they involve some major reorganizations in the linkages across functions within the U.S. industrial firm. The concern with improving design quality and manufacturability and with shortening design cycles to meet Japanese competition has led to significant efforts to bring together the people in product development and in production. While the importance of the Japanese pattern of moving people, and not just information, across functional lines has been widely recognized, the lower level of company control over individual careers and the greater level of career specialization in U.S. firms has meant that the widespread Japanese pattern of permanently moving researchers into production organizations as part of their career paths has not been feasible. However, firms are increasingly making use of cross-functional product development teams, with representatives of the various functions as full participants throughout the process, and the temporary assignment of R&D personnel to production units in order to follow the products they have designed right through the manufacturing process. In addition, some firms have begun to reexamine the criteria by which they select sites for manufacturing, opting in some cases for "co-location"—that is, putting product development and manufacturing at the same site, in order to facilitate cross-functional communication. These closer linkages between R&D and production have led to a reevaluation of the practice of locating manufacturing offshore in countries with low labor costs, at least for the pilot manufacturing facilities, as managers have come to recognize that the reduction in the wage bill may be more than offset by increased costs of maintaining linkages across functions.

Finally, the Japanese linkages across firms have drawn keen attention and increasing emulation in U.S. industry. The recent interest in the blurring of organizational boundaries by increasingly close networks with key suppliers and customers and with important sources of technology and the utilization of those networks in product development and process innovation attests to the growing recognition of the importance of learning networks in a dynamic competitive environment.[14] One of the idiosyncrasies of the legal system of the United States is that it is often easier for a U.S. firm to establish such linkages with foreign firms than with another U.S. firm.

The changes to date have been significant, far-reaching, and probably much greater than anyone would have foreseen a decade ago. However, not surprisingly, given the relatively short time since the full force of Japanese industrial competition was generally recognized, the changes are still largely reactive and are most evident in industries that have been directly affected by Japanese competition, such as autos, semiconductors, and computers. In both management practice and management theory, it has been the Japanese who have been most assiduous in exploring the implications of the growing importance of information in the industrial system. The constraints on learning imposed by U.S. management culture may be most significant not in preventing adaptive learning from Japanese best practice, but in restricting a leapfrogging of Japanese industrial practice and the development of distinctive and new approaches to the information-intensive industrial system. And constraints on changing that culture and on realizing innovations that emerge from those changes may, as some critics have suggested, be less an issue at the level of the firm than at the level of the industrial system as a whole.

THE CHALLENGE TO THE U.S. INDUSTRIAL SYSTEM

Of the four arenas of competition between firms in the United States and Japan—quality, productivity, product development, and price competitiveness—the last has been at the root of much of the involvement of U.S. industrial firms in the trade tensions between Japan and the United States. In many industries, U.S. firms allege that their Japanese counterparts can underprice them because of a wide variety of institutional factors that cannot be matched at the level of the firm. These include a lower cost of capital, due to government investment policies, the very high domestic savings rate, and the close networks between large firms and banks; a government bureaucracy and industrial system that has deliberately denied foreign firms entry to the Japanese market, thereby enabling Japanese firms to use the domestic markets as a source of profits to fund aggressive pricing elsewhere in the world; industrial groups that spread risk across firms; intellectual property laws and orientations allowing Japanese firms to avoid much of the cost of technology development;[15] "patient capital" from institutional shareholders; and a pattern of diversification of firms that enables them to cross-subsidize product lines. The merits of these challenges are still vigorously debated, and an assessment of their influence lies beyond the scope of this essay, but there is enough substance to make for a major challenge to the U.S. industrial system, especially to the role of the state in that system.

While the focus of the public debate over these institutional factors has been largely on the "unfair" advantages they confer on Japanese firms in price competition, however, their greatest importance may well lie in the stimulus they give to corporations to invest in continuing innovation in product development and production. Much of the dynamism of the Japanese industrial system over the last three decades has been ascribed to some combination of these factors, coupled with intense competition within the Japanese market that is mediated by government agencies concerned with preventing "excessive competition" that would cripple some or all of the firms in the industry.

Traditionally, the ideal role of the state in the U.S. industrial system has been focused not on preventing too much competition, but on forestalling too little—that is, regulating collusion among firms that would inhibit the organizing rights of labor, competition in pricing, and the entry of new firms into the industry. In other words, the primary role of the state has been to enforce the rights of labor and to protect the welfare of the consumer. However, the emerging industrial relations system offers relatively little scope for the state in its traditional role in the industrial relations system, and a growing body of critics argues that too great a concern for the citizen as consumer may be inimical to the long-run economic and industrial strength of the nation. On the other hand, the growing international competition offers a new role—ensuring an international "level playing field" on behalf of U.S. industry in two major contexts: trade negotiations and domestic policy.

In trade negotiations, the U.S. government is increasingly being asked to deny access to the U.S. market to firms from countries whose industrial systems give them "unfair" subsidies or protection, and to use its control of that access to force changes on the industrial systems of countries like Japan (including the other Asian economies, and perhaps in future the European Community). Exactly what constitutes an unfair practice is a matter of continuing and fierce controversy between the United States and its trading partners, and even within U.S. industry itself, but the demand for the government to assume this role is unlikely to lessen over the coming decade.

The domestic policy role is in providing support to make U.S. industry internationally competitive, and making international competitiveness a major consideration in the ongoing government interventions in the industrial system, from taxation to the efforts of local governments to attract foreign direct investment. However, while the voices urging the government to take a more active role in raising industrial competitiveness are growing in strength, considerable disagreement remains over the proper nature of that role.

The least controversial aspect of such a role involves raising the level of general education in the United States. In a system where tapping the knowledge of production workers is becoming increasingly important to innovation, the knowledge base, analytical skills, and capacity for sustained attention to problem solving are critically important, and few would deny that general U.S. education is behind that of its major trading partners, especially Japan, in this regard. But whether the very decentralized U.S. educational system is amenable to change is a problem that compounds the questions of what teaching method and substance would achieve the desired goals. Moreover, raising educational levels is a necessary but very long-term corrective.

A second aspect of the state's role in increasing international industrial competitiveness is that of facilitator for the creation of effective and efficient managerial networks. The removal or relaxation of antitrust laws, the increased use of government laboratories as a source of technology for private industry, and government consultation with industry on public policy issues are all steps that are being urged on the U.S. government from a wide variety of positions on the political spectrum.

Another arena affects international competitiveness but goes well beyond the role of the state: the definition of the corporation as a bundle of financial assets, discussed above as an element of managerial culture in the United States. A growing number of U.S. managers complain that while they personally would prefer to emphasize the knowledge-generating capacity of the firm, rather than the custody of its financial assets, as their key responsibility, they cannot bring about changes in behavior because of the nature of the U.S. industrial system as a whole. The financial definition of the firm is continuously reinforced in a system where managers find it easier to raise money from banks and financial markets for takeovers than for investment in new plants or in research, where the laws force boards of directors to put the interests of shareholders ahead of the interests of employees, and where firms are evaluated on their short-term financial performance. Even while recognition of the shortcomings of the system is growing, there is no clear program for change, or even a clear mapping of alternative courses of action.

Much of the recent writing on U.S. and Japanese industrial competition has a decidedly Darwinian tone. That is, it portrays the U.S. industrial system as a product of an earlier technological and international environment. In consequence, the system is being displaced by the later-developing Japanese system, which has managed over the last century to prevent U.S. industry from dominating its domestic environment and which thereby generated distinctive industrial patterns that are better adapted to the information-intensive environment that Japanese industry itself has done so much to create. Such an interpretation suggests that the U.S. industrial system must evolve to become more like the Japanese over time, or suffer the consequences of being "selected out" in the evolutionary process of the survival of the fittest. To date, the extent to which adaptive changes in U.S. industry have been shaped by responses to Japanese competition rather than by creative anticipation of future technological and social changes has done much to reinforce this view.

However, the learning across the Pacific has become a continuous two-way flow, rather than the one-way flow (from Japan to the United States) that a Darwinian model would lead us to expect. While U.S. management continues to try to grasp the essentials of "best practice" in production and product development in Japan, Japanese managers continue to try to learn from the way the United States organizes basic research and manages multinational operations. And even while the two systems continue to learn from one another, they continue to generate distinctive innovations that reflect the ongoing interactions of culture, institutions, and behavior within each society. The speed with which U.S. industry has responded to Japanese competition has been much greater than its critics allow, and provides a basis for optimism that the next stage of change in industrial firms and industrial systems in the United States will be more innovative and less reactive, providing even further scope for cross-societal learning.

NOTES

1. Bruce D. Henderson, "The Logic of Kanban," *Journal of Business Strategy* 6, no. 3 (1986), p. 12.
2. Steven C. Wheelwright, *Harvard Business Review* 59, no. 4 (1981), pp. 67–74.
3. For example, Philip Kotler, Liam Fahey, and Sankid Jatusripitak, *The New Competition* (Englewood Cliffs, N.J.: Prentice-Hall, 1985).
4. A recent addition to this literature has identified an important success factor in accounting, long considered one of the weak points of Japanese business: Toshiro Hiromoto, "Another Hidden Edge—Japanese Management Accounting," *Harvard Business Review* 66, no. 4 (1988), pp. 22–26.
5. See, for example, Jared Taylor, *Shadows of the Rising Sun* (New York: Quill, 1983); and S. Prakesh Sethi, Nobuaki Namiki, and Carl L. Swanson, *The False Promise of the Japanese Miracle* (Boston: Pitman, 1984).
6. For a good overview, see Robert Wood, Frank Hull, and Koya Azumi, "Evaluating Quality Circles: The American Application," *California Management Review* 26, no. 1 (1983), pp. 37–53.
7. R. Jaikumar, "Postindustrial Manufacturing," *Harvard Business Review* 64, no. 6 (1986), pp. 69–76.
8. Richard J. Schonberger and James P. Gilbert, "Just-in-Time Purchasing: A Challenge for U.S. Industry," *California Management Review* 26, no. 1 (1983), pp. 54–68.
9. D. Eleanor Westney, "Managing Innovation in the Information Age: The Case of the Building Industry in Japan" (Paper presented at the INSEAD conference on Managing Innovation, Fontainebleau, France, September 1987).
10. An interesting variant of this position asserts that the Japanese originally drew what is best about their industry and management (especially in quality control and personnel management) from U.S. management experts who were ignored at home, and that in learning from Japan, American managers are therefore learning from themselves, at one remove. See, for example, Leonard Nadler, "What Japan Learned from the U.S.—That We Forgot to Remember," *California Management Review* 26, no. 4 (1984), pp. 46–61.
11. The following discussion draws heavily on Thomas Kochan, Harry C. Katz, and Robert B. McKersie, *The Transformation of American Industrial Relations* (New York: Basic Books, 1986).
12. Ibid.
13. Reinhard Bendix, *Work and Authority in Industry* (Berkeley: University of California Press, 1956; repr. 1974), p. 326.
14. See, for example, Eric Von Hippel, *The Sources of Innovation* (New York: Oxford University Press, 1988).
15. For example, a patenting process that is based on the principle of "first to patent" rather than "first to invent," and a willingness among Japanese researchers to search for external technologies rather than to insist on developing their own—the relative absence of a "not-invented-here" syndrome.

5

JAPANESE CORPORATE CULTURE: LESSONS FROM FOREIGN DIRECT INVESTMENT

Haruo Shimada

Japanese direct investment in the United States has been increasing rapidly in the past several years. While the bulk of investment has been in financial assets and real estate, investment in manufacturing facilities and in service offices has also been growing markedly. Japanese direct investment in general, and in the last two categories in particular, offers an interesting social experiment: it furnishes an opportunity for examining the acceptability and workability of the technology, culture, and behavioral patterns of Japanese corporations as they encounter a different industrial society.

The experiences of Japanese firms so far have been mixed. On the one hand, their production technologies, with strong emphasis on human involvement, have been well accepted in the workshop and have yielded appreciable results. On the other hand, they are beginning to encounter frictions and conflicts in various social, cultural, and organizational dimensions of interactions.

In terms of economy and technology, Japanese direct investments in the United States have many obvious merits for Americans: they benefit consumers by providing commodities with greater competitiveness, producers by giving competitive stimulus, workers by opening employment opportunities, industries by offering technological transfer, host communities by creating tax revenues, and the country as a whole by increasing productive capacity.

However, some people and social groups are becoming increasingly skeptical about the impact of Japanese investment and at times have even become hostile toward it. Some resent the increasing presence of Japanese capital power in the American economy. They are becoming nervous about the growing share of Japanese ownership of American financial assets, corporations, and real estate. Some groups, such as small suppliers and trade unions, complain that Japanese investment does not bring them all the economic opportunities they think it should. Small suppliers claim that Japanese corporations investing in the United States order supplies from Japan or bring them to the United States, rather than ordering from local suppliers. Trade unions contend that Japanese companies are hiring many fewer workers than their American counterparts and that they are antiunion.

While a number of the complaints may reflect the uneasiness of Americans who are suffering from unfavorable economic conditions, the behavior and attitudes of some of the Japanese investors also seem responsible for such social resentment.

This essay discusses both the merits of Japanese investments and problematical attitudes of Japanese investors, and, in an effort to enhance understanding of key aspects of Japanese corporate culture, it explores background factors which have given rise to such attitudes.

JAPANESE DIRECT INVESTMENT IN THE UNITED STATES

The volume of Japanese overseas direct investment rose from $1–$4 billion in the late 1970s to greater than $33 billion in 1987, most of it in North America. As of 1987, the accumulated amount of investment reached $139 billion, of which $53 billion was in North America (including $15 billion invested in manufacturing alone). These increases have incited criticism and a negative reaction in the United States.

Merits of Foreign Direct Investment

With this dramatic rise in Japanese investment in the United States, the American public and specialists have increasingly focused attention on the impact on the U.S. economy and society. Some critics argue about the perils of Japanese dominance, while others point to the merits of introducing the capital necessary to promote economic activities. Economists tend to be of the latter school. Indeed, the economy gains in several obvious ways, including the following:

Benefit to consumers. Products manufactured as a result of Japanese direct investment often have greater competitiveness than those manufactured by domestic producers. American consumers can therefore obtain products of lower price, higher quality, or both.

Revitalization of industries. The inflow of foreign capital, particularly of productive resources, necessarily stimulates domestic competition. Through such competition, while less competitive firms and industries will lose their shares, more competitive ones will remain. Some firms and industries may even increase their productive efficiency because of the competition. In other words, growing foreign direct investment may help to stimulate and revitalize domestic industries in the United States by intensifying competition.

Favorable impact on employment. Direct investment creates employment opportunities related to the project. Whether foreign direct investment will also contribute to an increase in net employment opportunities for the economy will depend on several factors, such as the substitution of employment opportunities from the foreign direct investment for other such opportunities; the relative productivity of the foreign investment and other activities; and changes in overall economic growth, productivity, and the labor force. Unless the aggregate economy is stagnant, however, it is likely that new investment projects will create additional employment opportunities for the economy.

Technology transfer. Foreign direct investment projects accompanied by new or different technologies will provide learning opportunities, for certain technologies are likely to be transferred to the host country. The recent experiences of direct investment of Japanese manufacturing corporations in North

America suggest that technology transfer takes place successfully and effectively when it involves American production workers at the workplace.

Frictions and Conflicts

Despite the obvious benefits that foreign direct investment brings to the host country, such investment has engendered criticism and negative reaction. While few will deny the merits to consumers, many warn about the harmful effects of foreign investment on domestic producers, on workers, and even on the independence of technology. Critics argue that the inflow of foreign producers threatens and sometimes destroys the basis for survival of domestic producers. This view is often most loudly voiced by small producers, such as auto parts suppliers in the Detroit area. To the extent that they have political influence, these small producers can become a real force in the political dynamics of American society.

Trade unions warn that, since Japanese companies are more automated and work their employees harder than their American counterparts, they will provide fewer employment opportunities for the same amount of production than comparable American companies would. The unions also warn that Japanese investors will threaten employment opportunities for American union members, since they are antiunion.

Producers who wish to work with companies receiving Japanese investment often complain that Japanese firms bring their own suppliers or cooperating companies, and leave little opportunity for American suppliers to work with them. Japanese corporations often rebut these criticisms by pointing to the importance of fostering long-standing customer relationships to share information and jointly develop technology. Although some American companies are developing such relationships with Japanese investors, those without such access criticize Japanese corporations as being unfairly prejudiced and closed to outsiders.

In contrast to these criticisms and accusations, only a few years ago U.S. producers and trade unions, as well as the government, strongly solicited Japanese investment in the United

States. Americans insisted that Japanese firms manufacture products in the United States that they intend to sell there, rather than export these products from Japan. They even accused Japanese of being reluctant and hesitant in making such decisions. However, once the flow of direct investment began to grow drastically, negative reactions and criticism arose so rapidly in the United States as to overshadow the voice of welcome. What stands behind these changes, and what accounts for the mixed reactions within the United States?

A background factor that immediately comes to mind is the relative decline of American economic power. What is perceived to be a healthy stimulus in good times is no longer seen as such in bad times, but is viewed as a threat, particularly to the troubled sectors. Another factor is perhaps the absence of understanding of the nature of Japanese corporations and management. This lack of understanding may well have given rise to skepticism, unwarranted criticism and even perceptions of mysterious practices. Whatever the reasons, these mixed reactions are not independent of the pattern of behavior of Japanese corporations themselves. In the next section I examine some of the conspicuous behavioral patterns of Japanese corporations and consider if they are responsible for the mixed reactions in American communities and society.

PROBLEMS OF JAPANESE CORPORATE BEHAVIOR IN A DIFFERENT CULTURAL SETTING

Several problematic features are discernible in Japanese corporate behavior. I discuss six of them in this section: excessive competition; weak recognition of corporate citizenship; inappropriate use of local middle managers; unionization; dealing with minorities; and poor public relations strategies.

Excessive Competition

The inclination of Japanese corporations toward excessive competition has been criticized time and again not only by foreigners, but also by Japanese themselves. Little evidence, however, indicates that this competitive nature has diminished.

Fierce competition among many powerful Japanese corporations in foreign markets inevitably gives rise to dramatic increases in exports, direct investment, takeovers, and so forth.
This may very well disturb or distort the orderly market equi-
libria or transaction practices of foreign countries.

Weak Recognition of Corporate Citizenship

The idea of corporate citizenship is rarely discussed in the Japanese business community or, more broadly, in Japanese society.
In fact, this concept has only recently attracted explicit public
attention in Japanese industrial society, as Japanese corporations
have increased their investments abroad. It has not as yet been
well understood or digested by Japanese firms, however. In any
society, regardless of cultural norms, corporations are generally
expected to contribute in some way to their surrounding community, just as individuals are expected to participate in activities
for the good of the whole community.

In the case of Japanese society, however, the role of corporations in their surrounding community has rarely been explicitly
discussed, for a few good reasons. One is that the existence of a
corporation in a community is usually accepted as something
beneficial to the community, and the reason for its existence is
rarely questioned. Another is that the goals of a community's
social and political organizations often coincide with those of the
corporation. Japanese managers, therefore, naively tend to believe that what is good for the corporation must be good for the
community as well. Many Japanese executives believe that there
is no better contribution to their surrounding community than
to produce products that will sell well, since a prosperous company will be able to offer more employment opportunities and
tax revenues to the community. The relationship of the corporation with the community, however, obviously is not this simple.

Inappropriate Use of Local Middle Managers

Japanese companies operating in foreign countries do not appear to be successful in effectively utilizing local middle-level
managers and staff. Some may succeed, but what we hear about
overwhelmingly are unsuccessful experiences. What are the

symptoms? Foreign local personnel complain that the Japanese do not treat them as full-fledged members of the organization: they treat them as nothing more than guests. Thus, for example, Japanese subordinates will often report directly to headquarters in Japan, bypassing local supervisors; and important decisions are often made informally without involving local managers. These and other practices bother local staff. On the other hand, the Japanese complain that the foreign local managers do not—or do not try to—understand the basic premises of Japanese management, though they may claim or pretend to.

A natural consequence of such dissatisfaction on both sides is that foreign local managers do not stay long with Japanese companies. Unfortunately, the degree of commitment appears to correlate inversely with the level of their ability. Why, then, do able local people join Japanese firms operating in foreign countries? Many of them do so to learn new skills. Once they have achieved their goal, they leave the company and try to join other firms where they can work more comfortably, utilizing their experience and expertise.

With dissatisfaction and disenchantment on both sides, Japanese companies abroad cannot attract excellent human resources for local management. Even if they did, it would be temporarily, as the highest-caliber people would not stay long. This must be a great loss of opportunity from the viewpoint of Japanese corporations, because human resources are a critical asset for future development of Japanese corporations in the world market.

Unionization

Many Japanese companies operating abroad do not have unions—some because they have just started to operate and have not had the time to prepare to deal with unionization, others because they have set up plants or offices in areas where the union movement is largely absent, and still others because of their deliberate policy to avoid unionization.

It is notable that while most major companies in Japan are highly unionized, their foreign subsidiaries or transplants exhibit mixed attitudes toward unionization. Perhaps the majority of them are not unionized at this stage. Some that are enjoy cooperative and productive relationships with labor, while others have adversarial relationships.

The issue of unionization of Japanese companies abroad opens one of the most curious and sensitive questions to the industrial community of the host countries. Throughout the world, the perception is widely prevalent that most Japanese companies in Japan enjoy peaceful and productive labor-management relations. Also, there are many stories of the successful building of cooperative industrial relations within Japanese companies operating around the world. At the same time, however, another widely prevalent perception is that Japanese companies prefer to be nonunion and try to avoid unionization when they go out of the country, even though most of them are unionized in Japan.

This image provokes some delicate issues. One is that the growing direct investment by Japanese companies may increase the threat to the union movement in host countries because of their alleged antiunion inclination. Another is skepticism about the bona fide nature of Japanese unions. In my judgment, these arguments reveal serious misunderstandings. The bottom line for Japanese corporations concerning the question of unionization is whether the unions are willing to work productively with management to promote what I call humanware technology. This has been a strong point of the Japanese management throughout the process of developing industrial relations in the postwar economy.

The ambivalent attitude of Japanese corporations toward unionization in foreign countries reflects their anxieties, uncertainties, concerns, and lack of confidence in this area. Generally, no one can be certain about the outcome of any new challenge. A serious problem with Japanese management is its excessively defensive, awkward, closed, and inward-oriented position on this issue. Management should at least try to make efforts to have open and intensive dialogue with foreign unions, to see if the two sides can find common ground on which to work in the critical areas of their concerns. One must recognize, however, that although it may sound easy to do, the idea of having open dialogue and debate with outsiders is one of the most difficult cultural barriers for Japanese corporations to overcome.

Dealing with Minorities

Concern has been increasing in the United States that some of the Japanese invested companies are engaged in discriminatory employment practices. Critics argue that certain Japanese corporations operating in the United States are hiring many fewer blacks or women than they should, or are using some employment criteria by which such groups are less often chosen.

Japanese corporations under criticism assert that they are not violating the criteria of the Equal Employment Opportunity Commission (EEOC). In fact, careful examination reveals considerable gray areas in interpretation and actual implementation of EEOC rules and criteria. One major Japanese firm was accused of having engaged in discriminatory practices by imposing a maximum limit on commuting time, thereby, in effect, eliminating from the authorized zones of commutation some areas where minorities were more densely populated. Responding to this criticism, the company dropped the limit. The firm reportedly has settled the case with the EEOC by paying compensation.

It is, however, not so much the legal interpretation as the image of the corporation's behavior that is susceptible to such skepticism regarding discrimination. Ignorance or carelessness with regard to the minority issue is, in fact, deeply embedded in the structure of Japanese society. To the extent that this is the case, it is a formidable task for Japanese corporations to understand the meaning of the minority problem and cultivate a more sensitive attitude toward it.

Poor Public Relations Strategies

Japanese corporations operating abroad are quite underdeveloped in the area of public relations policies and strategies.

In fact, they spend considerable amounts of money in the public relations arena, buying air time on TV, as well as newspaper and magazine space for advertisements; hiring lobbyists with hopes of preventing unfavorable legislation from being drafted or passed; and making contributions in their host communities to help enrich school facilities, support charities, establish scholarships, and the like.

In spite of all this spending, however, they fail to make themselves understood well by the community and society. This drawback stems basically from their innate inward-looking and closed nature. They spend much effort explaining their corporation, production system, working conditions, philosophies, and so on to their employees, but only marginal efforts in explaining themselves to outsiders in the host society. They are open to casual tourists and visitors, but quite closed to serious journalists and researchers; consequently, there are few well-informed people who can articulately explain them to outside society. They pay some money to community activities, but they do not otherwise participate in such activities. They pay large amounts of money to political lobbyists, but they do not have appropriate human networks to ensure that the money is being effectively utilized for their corporate political purposes.

Developing effective public relations strategies in the American social and political environment, which is utterly different from Japanese society, presents new and challenging tasks for Japanese corporations. They have a long way to go in developing such strategies.

BACKGROUND OF JAPANESE CORPORATIONS

Having examined various conspicuous behavioral patterns of Japanese corporations that appear to be responsible, at least partially, for mixed reactions against Japanese companies in American industrial society, let me propose my hypothesis about background factors that inevitably generate misunderstandings and conflicts when different cultures meet in the arena of direct investment.

Homogeneous versus Heterogeneous Societies

The homogeneity of Japanese society is often contrasted in this context with the heterogeneity of American society, well-known as a "nation of immigrants." Although there are many scientific problems in making such a sweeping simplification as to characterize Japanese society as homogeneous, it is undeniably more homogeneous than American society.

This relative homogeneity—and, perhaps more important, the Japanese perception of homogeneity of their own society— gives rise to important behavioral patterns in Japanese corporations. The fact that Japanese managers do not understand or appreciate the meaning of corporate citizenship is closely related to this perception of homogeneity. While they can understand theoretically that American society is a heterogeneous one, consisting of people with different racial, regional, and religious backgrounds and commitments, it is hard for them to internalize this understanding to the point of modifying their own spontaneous responses and reactions. The lack of sensitivity of Japanese management and corporations to the issue of minorities is also related to this perception.

The perceived homogeneity of the Japanese society reinforces the inward-looking attitude of Japanese corporations. This characteristic of organizational behavior significantly affects Japanese managerial attitudes toward foreign local middle-level managers, unions, and minorities. Management's inward-oriented attitude also hampers the development of effective public relations strategies, which are, by definition, outward-oriented.

Government Policies

The way government policies are made exerts significant influence on the behavioral patterns of corporations. It can determine the government-business relationship somewhat directly through industrial policies; it can determine the nature of corporate behavior indirectly by structuring the capital market; and it can influence, though more indirectly, the basic premises of the structure of the industrial society.

Japanese government has played a critical role in fostering the growth of modern industries during the process of industrialization that began in the mid-nineteenth century; during the early postwar period, it had substantial effect on businesses through its powerful industrial policies.

In contrast to the U.S. government, the Japanese leadership carefully orchestrated industrial organization in such a way that the existence of a good number of major companies was assured for each industry so that they could compete quite fiercely under both direct and indirect controls of the government. This structure of competition is often described as oligopolistic competition; its gimmick is that it claims to attain two seemingly contradictory goals simultaneously, namely, fierce competition among companies and their assured survival. After a decade, or at most two, the control of government diminished markedly. But this peculiar structure of market competition has persisted.

This "excessive competition" is reinforced also through another indirect channel of government control: monetary policy. During the early phase of postwar development, the government imposed strict control over interest rates for the purpose of providing funds at low cost to export-oriented industries. Major corporations of such industries were financed through massive bank loans endorsed indirectly by the government. Although the degree of the government's control and influence has diminished significantly with the subsequent development of the economy, this early modeling of the structure of the capital market and the mode of corporate finance left important imprints on the behavioral pattern of Japanese corporations: they are more concerned with maintaining or increasing market shares—that is, with excessive competition—than with profit rates. This is not surprising, because insofar as corporations can be financed largely by bank loans, whose interest rates are more or less fixed and controlled by the government, they do not have to worry about profit or dividend rates to attract investors.

Another important effect of the dominant role of the government in Japanese industrial society was the historical conformity of the goals of the corporation with the goals of government, both aimed at mobilizing all resources for the purpose of industrial development of the country. In fact, under this supreme goal, the purposes of all social and economic organizations—the government, corporations, regional and local organizations, social groups, and even families and individuals—were assimilated. In other words, the government in effect established the basic structure of Japanese society.

Although this model worked only for a limited period during the development of the Japanese economy, it may well have had a certain effect on the value system of the people and on their behavioral patterns. To the extent that this was the case, it is not surprising that Japanese corporations have not developed the sensitivity necessary to deal with heterogeneous groups that have different values and that resolve conflicts openly, discuss and debate with outsiders, formulate effective public relations strategies, bargain with the government, and so forth. Being well-sheltered by the government's control, they had no need to tackle these issues on their own.

CONCLUSIONS

The recent experience of massive foreign direct investment by Japanese firms has provided us with interesting data regarding the nature of their corporate culture.

Mixed reactions in American industrial society toward Japanese investments suggest an interesting dichotomy between the relatively successful experience of technology transfer to production workers and the somewhat problematic managerial, social, political, and cultural interactions.

While negative reactions stem to some extent from specific background factors of the American economy and society, peculiar patterns of Japanese corporate behavior also are responsible for misunderstandings and conflicts.

I began with the hypothesis that many aspects of the peculiar Japanese corporate behavior stem from deeply embedded perceptions of homogeneity of the Japanese society and from the historical inheritance of the powerful and critical role of the Japanese government in the process of industrialization. To the extent that this is the case, as Japanese companies globalize their activities, they increasingly face major challenges to remodel their traditional corporate culture in response to fundamental structural changes of economic and social environments, and to adapt to new experiences of working with people of different cultures.

On the structural side, with the increasing globalization of corporate activities, the control and influence of the government diminishes. But at the same time, governmental protection also declines. This means that while they can enjoy more freedom, Japanese corporations will have to make decisions more at their own risk than before. Corporations will also have to deal with younger cohorts in the work force who have different ideas from the generation that promoted postwar industrialization under a peculiar industrial culture. Moreover, the nature of the work force will become increasingly heterogeneous with the growing participation of women and workers with a variety of backgrounds.

Experience in working abroad will have a powerful impact on the Japanese people and corporations. They have been operating for a long time in an environment where the homogeneity of people and their ideas is assumed. Now they learn through their day-to-day operations, and sometimes at considerable cost, that they have to work with people with different ideas, cultures, and backgrounds. They must realize that in the past they had a somewhat biased view of the nature of people. This recognition of heterogeneity of people will inevitably change the attitudes and behavior of people and corporations in the long run.

As they accumulate experience working in foreign communities where the diversity of values and attitudes of social groups is much more pronounced than in Japanese industrial communities, and the influence of the central government is much less pervasive, Japanese corporations will more keenly learn the meaning and significance of behaving as a corporate citizen in the making of the community. If they wish to be a part of the society where they operate, they will have to share the responsibilities as well as the goals of the society. They cannot escape from the problems; they have to join the common endeavor to improve the situation. This is what corporate citizenship means. With greater experience, Japanese corporations will and should learn this lesson.

6

INSTITUTIONAL CHANGES IN THE U.S. POLICY PROCESS: BUREAUCRATS AND POLITICIANS

Bert A. Rockman

This essay is about the relationship that has evolved in the United States between its politicians and its bureaucrats. The relationship is a complex one because almost nothing about American government is simple or straightforward. Indeed, from the complexity of the government, a great deal follows.

First, the ways in which bureaucrats and politicians connect—or often fail to—is distinctive in the United States because of the division of authority and power that stems from the constitutional doctrine of checks and balances. Traditional career bureaucrats in executive departments and agencies generally have been moved further and further from channels of political access in the executive. Both the White House and the Congress have acted to place politically appointed specialists in positions that in Japan (or most any other place) would go to career officials. The rise of professional staffs in both the presidency and the Congress is the product of the post-1945 modernization of the federal government, the development of presidential centrism, and the congressional response to that development. These staffs give each branch of government independent expertise to bolster competing policies. Moreover, the development of noncareer professional staffs in the executive and the legislature reinforce the institutional division of authority that makes impossible a unified civil service able to serve all the branches of government.

Second, the partisan division of government that has been a fact of political life in Washington for most of the last three and a half decades creates especially complicated issues of accountability and loyalty between career officials and politicians. In recent years, accountability-forcing micromanagement from within the executive and also from Congress has narrowed the discretion that civil servants have been able to exercise in implementing policy. Republican presidential administrations generally have been suspicious of a career civil service they believe (to some extent, accurately) is not wholly in accord with their more laissez-faire philosophy of government. This helps explain why, with Republicans controlling the White House for most of the past 40 years, the latitude of civil servants has narrowed.

Third, the present policy climate in Washington also has restricted opportunities for program promotion and growth. Management, rather than program entrepreneurship, is now the key element in the career official's job description. To many bureaucrats, this situation is not very attractive because they have fewer opportunities for creativity.

Fourth, while in any political system bureaucrats act as stabilizers, the immensely complex American system itself adds much ballast, because a government built upon the idea of conflicting constituent interests and institutional prerogatives cannot be expected to easily shift direction. As a result, and especially in the context of partisan division, professional noncareer staff personnel have become more important and career civil servants less so.

Finally, in considering how the United States and Japan interact, one must be aware of significant differences between the processes and structures of governing in the two countries. While it is not self-evident how these differences affect the quality of governance in each country, the long-term hold of the Liberal Democratic Party (LDP) on power in Japan provides greater continuity to governing there and a longer-term view than would be the case in the more openly conflictual American governing process. The implications of this are explored in the concluding section.

BUREAUCRATS AND POLITICIANS IN THE UNITED STATES—AN IDIOSYNCRATIC RELATIONSHIP

The relationship between bureaucrats and politicians in American government is complicated by American political institutions—in particular, the sharing of political authority that results from having a legislature independent of the executive. The bureaucrat-politician relationship is complicated also by the rise in numbers, but especially in importance, of a third set of players in government—congressional and White House staff. Strictly speaking, these personnel do not fit into categories conveniently labeled "bureaucrat" or "politician," although they share some traits with each. Both presidential and congressional staff members, for example, have a striking amount of policy expertise and specialized knowledge. However, they also have political or institutional patrons, whom they serve not with detached neutrality but with the expectation that they are more or less exclusively in service to the interests and goals of those patrons. The prominence of this new breed of policy/political hybrid is in part a function of increased policy and political demands on the institutions they work for (the presidency and the Congress). Most important, though, their presence reflects the reality of a government whose principal policymaking institutions are essentially in conflict with one another.

By the time George Bush's term is at an end in 1993, two-thirds of the previous 40 years will have been spent under conditions of divided government. Assuming their continued control of the House of Representatives, in all these years the Democrats will have dominated at least one chamber of the Congress; if they maintain their majority in the Senate too, for all but six of these years they will have held both. The closer we come to the present, the more stark is the nature of this division. During the last two decades of American political life, the government has been divided for sixteen years. The normality of this situation conditions American politicians (and bureaucrats) to the expectation that anything else is anomalous. Divided government has had a profound impact on the relationship between bureaucrats and politicians in the United States, and it certainly is one of the important contributing factors to the emergence of presidential and congressional staff personnel.

THE DEVELOPMENT OF WHITE HOUSE AND CONGRESSIONAL STAFFS

Any effort to understand bureaucrat-politician relations in the United States requires at the outset an appreciation of the roles of staff personnel and the reasons for the development of those roles. It also requires an understanding that these noncareer professionals have come to perform functions that politicians are reluctant to delegate to career bureaucrats.

Postwar Modernization of the Federal Government

Chastened by the economic crisis of the 1930s and the military mobilization of the 1940s, the American federal government in the immediate post-1945 world began a structural modernization. The new U.S. role in the world and the changes in the size and functions of the federal government that had been under way over the dozen years since the Depression and during the war provided a strong impetus to generate new governmental institutions and procedures. Within a very short time, a number of laws were passed to augment the machinery of American government and to lay the groundwork for expansive staffing arrangements. The Congressional Reorganization Act (1946), the Administrative Procedures Act (1946), the National Security Act (1947), and even the Full Employment Opportunities Act (1946) all created new functions for government, new units within which the work of government would take place, and substantial increases in staffing. Congress rationalized its committee structure and created more elaborate staffing patterns around it—though none as elaborate as those existing at present. The White House, too, had mechanisms created for it that professionalized national security and military advice, as well as macroeconomic advice. The role of the Washington staffer, if still only in blurred outline, had begun to emerge.

Presidential Centrism

By the time Richard Nixon took office in 1969, the President's staff clearly was viewed as a resource for keeping decisions in the White House, for maximizing presidential discretion, and for minimizing the politics of constituencies, press leaks, and the influence of cabinet secretaries' own agendas. The White House staff did not increase dramatically in numbers under Nixon, but it did grow dramatically in importance. During the Kennedy and Johnson years, academicians such as McGeorge Bundy and Walt W.

Rostow added outside perspectives and academic status to the newly developing role of the Special Assistant to the President for National Security Affairs—a role that earlier had been much less influential and occupied by career military and foreign service officers on secondment. Under Nixon, however, Henry Kissinger gave the role the status of key foreign policy conceptualizer. Above all, Kissinger enlarged the professional staff serving under the National Security Adviser to about 60 officials, some on temporary assignment from the military, the foreign service, or intelligence agencies, and others from the world of universities and research institutes.

While the Kissinger model serves only to exemplify staff prominence, the real question is what was driving the development of this White House staff apparatus. Aside from Nixon's now well-known idiosyncrasies and penchant for secrecy, it is crucial to focus on larger structural changes in the American system of governance. Nixon was the first Republican president to enter office in the twentieth century with a Democratic Congress. Dwight Eisenhower began with a Republican Congress, although he later had to deal with Democratic Congresses. But Eisenhower operated in an environment in which, particularly on foreign policy, the Democratic leadership was more sympathetic to him than was his own party's leadership. This was the so-called, if indeed very anomalous, era of bipartisan foreign policy.

Nixon, however, came into office with the numbers stacked heavily against him in both the Senate and the House, and with little proclivity to deal with the Congress. Rather, his style, repeated with far greater sophistication by Ronald Reagan, was to deal with Congress as little as possible and to govern as much as possible through executive means, essentially through the White House or the Executive Office of the President. Certainly, this mode of operation was designed to minimize dealing with and through the cabinet departments. Congress passes, monitors, funds, and amends the laws under which the departments operate, thereby having a strong influence over their policies and programs. Moreover, both directly and through congressional committees or subcommittees, the departments are linked to external constituencies with interests in the maintenance of the status quo. The Nixon White House thus was concerned that departmental secretaries would inevitably be spokesmen for their departmental or congressional agendas instead of for the White House agenda. This concern was exacerbated by the fact that the Nixon White House viewed senior career officials as hostile to its policies and sympathetic to its political enemies.

Congressional Change and Challenge

After winning an overwhelming electoral victory in 1972, yet one in which Democrats retained control of the Congress, President Nixon appeared to recognize that not everything could be done directly from the presidential office. Consequently, instead of bringing the executive branch into the White House, he began to bring the White House into the executive branch. With some notable exceptions (Henry Kissinger, for example), the President appointed relatively unknown and weak cabinet officials, and layered underneath them loyalists who had served him in the presidency during his first term and who could operate inside the departments as his eyes and ears. The strategy was to try to control the departments on-site instead of directly through the White House. This strategy, which came to be brilliantly executed during the Reagan administration, was later called "the administrative presidency." Nixon's objective of controlling policy was unchanged; only the means for achieving it were different.

The Watergate episode and the threat of impeachment brought to a temporary halt all of these strategies to transform the executive branch into a presidential branch. At the same time, the challenges issued to the Congress's institutional prerogatives and political interests by the Nixon style of governance, and the retrospective concern about inadequate consultation with Congress before the United States was plunged into the Vietnam War, had combined with changes on Capitol Hill to bring forth a great rush of reform. However, while some of the reforms strengthened the policy capabilities of the Congress, others diffused its power, thus weakening its ability to act.

Older members of Congress, especially in the House of Representatives, were being replaced, which meant a major shift of institutional power. The pace of this displacement accelerated rapidly as a result of retirements induced by the generous congressional pension law of 1973 and the election of large numbers of new, reform-minded Democrats in 1974.

Moreover, each party was in the process of coalescing around a more distinct political philosophy, and thus more conflict was created across party lines. In addition, the majority (Democratic) party caucus in the House both strengthened control over its members and distributed influence more evenly within the chamber. The consequence was to strengthen the party role in the legislative agenda yet also empower the party rank and file members to a far greater extent. Precipitating this latter development, the Democrats in the House earlier had created a bill of rights for subcommittees, giving them their own staffs and thereby enlarging the staff role in the chamber. An important effect was to further spread leadership authority and policy resources around as more than two-fifths of the House Democrats would become chairmen of subcommittees, putting substantial expert resources at their disposal in battles for control of policy.

THE GREAT DIVIDE—THE PARTISAN SPLIT IN GOVERNMENT

The great staffing boom, then, developed around the following circumstances: Presidents, particularly Nixon and Reagan, wanted to convert the executive branch into a presidential branch so that as much governing as possible could be done through the executive (and especially the White House) with minimal congressional approval or oversight. Meanwhile, Congress moved simultaneously—and perhaps contradictorily—to circumscribe the growth of presidentialism and to enhance its own power through strengthened in-house analytical and intelligence expertise, on the one hand, and to buy off a more demanding membership by diffusing that power among more majority party members, on the other. The crucial factor underlying this intensifying competition between the branches of government was that it was occurring under divided party control of the government, a condition that, to a somewhat lesser extent, also would confront the Reagan presidency.

The more or less permanent state of "combat readiness" that marks divided government means it is undesirable from the White House point of view for those who work for the executive to be responsive also to congressional policy preferences that may differ from the administration's. Moreover, career officials are seen as having biases that they seek to lock into long-term support for their programs. Staff personnel, on the contrary, are impermanent; they are "in and outers" with loyalties to their present bosses, whom they typically serve at the latter's discretion. Often, staff personnel are a good bit younger than their career counterparts in the executive branch. Because it is easier to exert influence in a small shop than in a large factory, bright young staffers enjoy some of the freewheeling discretion that can be exercised only in small group settings (such as the White House or policy levels of executive departments or on congressional staffs), but that is inhibited by the more formalistic environment of the large bureaucratic offices of cabinet departments. Moreover, because of their impermanent status, staffers are inclined to be more responsive in the short term to their political patrons than career officials might be. Appointed staffers do not have to ask themselves what the next set of superiors will think, or how present decisions constrain distant options, since their principal service is to a particular political patron. This does not mean that staffers are likely to be more parochial in their views than career bureaucrats—sometimes they are decidedly less so. It does mean that they are less likely to consider the sorts of options that will confront their patrons' successors.

In other political systems the offices of the head of government, of the parliament, and of the cabinet ministers are typically staffed with a small number of people who almost always are civil servants. In the United States both the Office of the President and the Congress are staffed far more extensively than their counterparts in other countries. And while the presidential staff has some civil servants, there is virtually no tradition to include them as policy advisers; those who are there mostly serve in third-echelon positions in White House support agencies. No such career service even exists in the Congress, which does not subject itself to civil service personnel rules.

As a result, the career bureaucracy has been a major loser among the players in the Washington governing system. The staff buildup on both ends of Pennsylvania Avenue provides resources for each institution—the Congress and the presidency—when the confrontational spirit becomes prominent. In the end, the White House and the Congress must cooperate if much is to get done. But because they are separate actors and are elected fundamentally by separate electorates, they are not, so to speak, in the same boat. As a consequence, even though many staff members, if not most, are fully qualified professionals, they tend to see things from the particular perspectives of their institutional or personal patrons. Moreover, whereas the President wants to have things done his way, there is no *the way* in Congress, with its two equally but differently powerful chambers and its enormously decentralized and diffused authority.

There is slight personnel movement from one branch to the other. Sometimes disgruntled bureaucrats, often foreign service officers, leave the executive and find a political patron in Congress. Congressional staffers also move into the executive but tend to do so at the beginning of Democratic administrations. Overall, though, the American system has no unified civil service to staff both the presidency and the Congress, as might be expected in other systems.

Accountability and Loyalty within the Executive Branch

To understand some of the mismatches in intergovernmental dealings, especially between the United States and a country such as Japan, where the bureaucracy has been (and largely remains) the locus of tremendous power, it is worth exploring in somewhat greater depth why the position of senior career bureaucrats in the U.S. executive branch has diminished.

It is important to come back to the conditions of divided government. In the United States, the executive departments are accountable not only to the Chief Executive (the President) but also to the Congress, which, as mentioned earlier, authorizes the legislation under which the departments function, appropriates the funds they spend, and oversees and reviews their performance. If presidents want to achieve their goals, and especially if they are of a different party than the congressional majority, they have two routes open to them: a competitive but accommodative bargaining game in which the risks of governing are syndicated (in a parliamentary system we would call this a grand coalition); or a confrontational game in which minimum cooperation is engendered and where each player tries to get away with the maximum within the short term. For a variety of reasons, the first of these options is not often taken even when presidents and congressional majorities are of the same party, as was the case in the Carter administration. Competition between the branches seems to outweigh all other considerations. But the fact of party division seems to condition presidents to try especially hard to move ahead without giving ground in advance. While in his early months in office President Bush is apparently trying to work cooperatively with a Democratic Congress, the President, unlike a prime minister, is under no particular obligation to consult anyone at all.

Efforts at short-run power plays also create conflicts between the President and Congress in the longer run. And partially for this reason, these circumstances create potential conflict between the President and the senior career bureaucracy. As noted earlier, administrations more often than not view senior career bureaucrats—who are directly, yet not exclusively, accountable to them—as linked to Congress, especially through staffs on the relevant committees and subcommittees. They perceive these bureaucrats' loyalty to be divided in a variety of ways: to their programs, to the constituencies of these programs (which include members of Congress), and to their intellectual commitment to policies that are at odds with the administration's, especially if the administration is a Republican one. To some degree, all of these perceptions are valid.

For example, senior career bureaucrats in the executive departments frequently have more personal contact with Congress than with the cabinet secretaries or other administrative department heads. In parliamentary systems, typically, the contact route works the other way: the senior career official is located closer to the minister (who normally is also a member of parliament), and contacts are mediated through the latter. In some parliamentary systems with particularly active and powerful parliamentary bodies—West Germany and Italy, for example, or Japan when the Diet is in session—senior career bureaucrats are engaged both with their ministers and with parliamentarians. Only in the United States do career bureaucrats have more contact with political authorities outside their organizations than with the political leaders at the top of their departmental hierarchies. It is not uncommon for a senior career official to serve through the entire tenure of a cabinet secretary without ever meeting the secretary one-on-one or in a small group.

Two factors explain this situation: first, cabinet secretaries frequently prefer to rely on their subcabinet political appointees, who are layered over the senior career officials; those appointees, in turn, may be exceptionally suspicious of the career executives. Second, Congress represents a lifeline to bureaucrats who more often have reason to fear changes imposed by the executive than by Congress. In particular, Congress has the power at the very least, through its committees and subcommittees, to make life difficult or embarrassing for those appointees who have mandated changes that may rub the bureaucrats— and, above all, the relevant congressional committee or subcommittee—the wrong way. To senior career officials, therefore, Congress is a good line of defense, especially since it takes only a small number of congressional staff personnel or members to be roused into action to disrupt changes imposed by the presidential appointees.

Because of the multiple linkages that senior career officials have, and because of the multiple sources of their accountability (the Constitution, Congress and its statutes, and departmental authority), the presidential administration in power often views senior careerists as prime suspects for disloyal behavior. Key presidential staff frequently see senior career officials as disposed to make alliances with key members of Congress and interest groups in opposition to administration initiatives, thus subverting them. Whether such behavior actually occurs or, especially, to what extent it occurs is a lot less relevant to relations between political appointees and career officials than the perception that it can and does occur. A presidential administration that comes to office with the belief that the civil service represents an impediment to its plans will plot to do all it can to seal off the senior career officials from other channels of political influence or, at least, to remove them as much as possible from the action. As a result, most of the recent administrations have concentrated decision-making and discretion among the political appointees in the departments and among the central clearance operations of the presidential office. In the present environment, senior civil servants are expected to be managers, not advisers; increasingly, they are to be told not only what to do but exactly how to do it.

Micromanagement as an Accountability-Forcing Tool

In Washington, this increasingly narrowed conception of the role of the senior civil servant is being implemented through a process called micromanagement, which effectively removes discretion from the administrative agency. The development of micromanagement is the direct result of clashes within the executive branch and between presidential administrations and the Congress. In recent times, and especially during the Reagan administration, the presidential staff agency, the Office of Management and Budget, has played a powerful role in defining how an agency should implement a law in accordance with presidential policy interests. Political heads of the implementing agencies also have made decisions to implement laws exclusively in accordance with presidential preferences or perceived presidential preferences.

Administrative interpretation is one way a presidential administration can try to control the executive branch. But since Congress writes the statutes under which these interpretations are made, it, too, retains a proprietary interest in the way the law is being carried out. The most direct way for Congress to ensure that its laws will not be implemented in ways contrary to its preferences is to tighten the screws so that an agency retains little discretion. Congress rarely wants to punish the career officials.

(Indeed, the senior career bureaucrats often welcome such intrusions, partly because they are usually more comfortable with the status quo and are often unsympathetic to changes imposed from within the executive branch.) What the Congress does want to do, however, is to restrict the range of action available to the presidential administration and its appointees. Nonetheless, this process also necessarily limits the latitude for civil servants' action. As a result, presidential constraints on bureaucratic initiative are compounded by congressional constraints.

The Political and Policy Preferences of Senior Civil Servants

The view, particularly of Republican presidential administrations, that career civil servants (especially those at a "policy level") are not sympathetic to their designs has some basis in fact. During the Nixon years, the President complained that the senior career service was politically opposed to his agenda. It is not possible to infer whether such alleged lack of sympathy actually translated into opposition. But the fact is that only small minorities of senior career officials (and an even smaller minority of foreign service officers) identified their political preferences as Republican. On the basis of a variety of attitudes as well as party identification measures, it is fair to conclude that Nixon was correct in believing that the bureaucracy he faced was considerably to the left of his administration.[1]

By the mid-1980s, substantial change had overtaken the senior civil service, which, by then, was more evenly split in its political affiliation. It was, in fact, much further to the right than it had been during the Nixon period, yet it was still not nearly as far to the right as the Reagan administration itself was on policy preferences, especially with respect to the role of government. In other words, the right-of-center Nixon presidency faced a left-leaning bureaucracy, whereas the much further right Reagan presidency faced a centrist or even mildly right-center career bureaucracy.[2] Although, with major exceptions, particularly in environmental regulation and preservation, the Reagan administration thus operated in a bureaucratic environment less hostile to its objectives, neither administration had the level of responsiveness it desired. In any event, the view among Republican presidents is that the career bureaucracy is potentially aligned with their political foes and must be monitored accordingly.

Any presidential administration, whatever its political coloration, comes into office wanting to make change. How much change it seeks depends upon the instincts of the President and the coalition that carried him into office. Anywhere and everywhere, however, bureaucrats tend to be suspicious of abrupt departures from the status quo, whatever that status quo is; incremental changes can be handled more satisfactorily. Often where politicians see opportunities, bureaucrats see obstacles. This is partly because bureaucrats, perhaps more frequently than politicians, are forced to deal with affected groups and, thus, become entangled within a web of prevailing interests. Consequently, even the Democratic administration of President Carter viewed Washington as a city bogged down in narrow-minded concerns. It therefore came to office with strong antipathies toward the bureaucracy, especially toward what it often saw as the nexus of interests connecting bureaucrats and congressional subcommittees.

An obvious implication here is that the more any administration wants to make change and the more committed it is to doing so, the more it will induce skepticism from—and be skeptical toward—the bureaucracy. Under such circumstances, therefore, the more an administration will build in staffing mechanisms to skirt traditional bureaucratic venues.

In general, Republican presidents see the bureaucracy as favorable to their political foes because the administrative apparatus mushroomed under Franklin D. Roosevelt in the 1930s. Whereas in other societies the state bureaucracy was associated with conservative elites and the preservation of a hierarchical social order, in the United States bureaucratic development was associated with controversial social reform and economic interventionism, and with the Democratic Party, which controlled the apparatus during its formative years.

The Republican ideology of a low-tax, low-social-spending state thus lends itself to questioning the legitimacy and purposes of the bureaucracy although, for the most part, actual practice necessarily leads to its acceptance.

Missions and Roles in the Current Policy Environment

Putting ideology and politics aside, however, the current environment of budgetary austerity clearly has led to a shift in the priorities of government. New initiatives that cost money are not high on the agenda of either party or either branch of government. Even so, outlays continue to claim a growing share of the gross national product, especially for so-called noncontrollable expenditures, such as the exploding cost of servicing the recently incurred large budget deficits. The effect is to constrain the amounts of discretionary income that the government might otherwise have available for new programs or for providing more support to existing ones.

One result of this is that senior program bureaucrats have fewer substantive challenges and entrepreneurial incentives. Their problems are managerial ones, and even there they often have less room for maneuver. To a considerable degree, therefore, it is the senior bureaucrats who manage programs or regulations who feel the loss of influence most keenly.

This environment promotes a redistribution of bureaucratic influence from those who wish to gain resources to those who wish to control them. So, while the Reagan administration treated senior career bureaucrats in the spending departments as potential enemies, one Reagan adviser, Martin Anderson, in a recent book dealing with the Reagan administration's preparations for taking office, noted that the White House took senior bureaucrats in the Office of Management and Budget into its confidence and let them go to work on identifying targets for budget cuts.[3]

While changes in the agenda of government have affected some bureaucratic roles more profoundly and adversely than others, the general effect of divided and clashing government has been steady politicization. The barriers between department heads and senior careerists have thickened. The departments themselves have ceded power to central monitoring and coordinating agencies within the Office of the President. And those presidential agencies, in turn, increasingly bear the marks of politicization.

In the context of divided government, the incentives for executive and congressional politicians are clear. Presidents and their entourages want to control the executive branch in order to make it responsive only to presidential wishes. On the other side, the congressional majority needs to be well armed to combat presidential incursions into its territory, which includes oversight of the functions and performance of the executive branch. The executive branch, in other words, is not a no-man's-land; it is more like everyone's land. It is the *joint* property of the President and the Congress.

In the face of these divisions, bureaucrats are a stable force. Like other stable forces, though, they are perceived by incoming presidential administrations as committed to the status quo in both program and institutional terms. Presidents come into office trying to move mountains, and bureaucrats look like one of the mountains. Impermanent staffs, on the other hand, can perform for politicians those functions they think they need to have performed for them. Presumably, staffs can bring assets of expertise or political skill without the burdens of past commitments or divided loyalties based on the expectation that they will have to serve others. Not surprisingly, they have become more important as line bureaucrats have become less so.

In a more politically serene setting, such as Japan, the experience, stability, and at least formal neutrality of the bureaucracy would seem to be virtues. But that is not necessarily so in the United States (although it may seem so to professors of public administration). To American politicians, especially those of the executive branch, experience implies prior commitments, stability means links and alliances forged with other (potentially opposition) elements on the Washington scene, and the expectation of neutrality suggests a lack of commitment and fervor on behalf of present (administration) goals.

If bureaucrats add ballast to governing—and a reasonable amount of cold water to dash foolish enthusiasms—that addition is not always appreciated by politicians with strong ideas (or powerful constituencies). It is reasonable, of course, to infer that a government lacking in stabilizing forces will suffer discontinuities and significant lapses in prudent judgment. Nonetheless, the reality is that bombast frequently overpowers ballast.

COMPLEXITY, RESPONSIBILITY, AND CONFLICT

The complexity of the American system overall often compensates for this imbalance to some degree, adding the ballast that more powerful civil service systems provide in other countries. For example, because of its diffuse power and cumbersome procedures, the Congress in a sense often adds stability, if not always prudence, to the policy and institutional relationships in Washington. Still, presidents have the ability to act as a single force. They can—where Congress often cannot—be decisive in their behavior. And when experienced and prudential bureaucratic judgments are removed from presidential deliberations, or from the milieus of their cabinet secretaries, the result can be injudicious and risky behavior in both policy and political terms.

Looked at from an institutional perspective, the willingness of presidents to engage in risky behavior is not purely a consequence of the eclipse of the senior civil service; it also is a cause of executive politicization.

There is no question, of course, that politicians ultimately are responsible for governing, and their judgments and directions must prevail. The terms on which this is done are crucial, however. For example, the stage at which political considerations enter in becomes paramount: it is one thing to make political judgments with the benefit of expert opinion; it is quite another to dictate what should be done without the benefit of such advice. Strong theories or "ideologies" have had a decided advantage in Washington; their proponents have generally operated on the premise (or the hope) that the "facts" will follow to buttress their ideas. In this setting, bureaucrats, who are likely to be skeptical empiricists and weak theorists, have little chance to voice their concerns or, in any case, to get a reasonable hearing. Thus, the cause and the consequence of politicization of the executive (its "presidentialization," so to speak) is that ideas are not generally expected to be tested by facts, but rather facts are to be stylized to accord with strong ideas.

As to the terms on which civil servants and politicians coexist, it is worthwhile for a moment to contrast the United States and Japan. In the United States, control of the apparatus of political authority is continuously competitive; in Japan, though it has been under increasing pressure, a single party has governed almost continuously for about three and a half decades. In the first case, clash and conflict between the political authorities often exist, with bureaucrats caught in the middle and increasingly wary of political interventions; in the second, the divide of partisan politics within the government is inconsequential, and even though there is a need to deal with opposition political maneuvering and questioning in the Diet, and despite factional competition within the ruling party, the administrative apparatus and the LDP show a substantial degree of cooperation. This predictability of the Japanese bureaucrats' environment, in contrast to that of their American counterparts, makes for a much less defensive way of accommodating to it and, with the politicians' general lack of independent resources and expertise, reinforces the bureaucrats' strong role in the policy process.

The Madisonian system of partitioning political authority has many virtues. But it can accentuate conflict, and when the conditions are ripe for that to happen, the career bureaucrats are caught in the middle. Their influence in the executive diminishes, while their relations with Congress further solidify. Ultimately, however, playing the political game with Congress is a sign of defensive tactics employed by career officials whose programs are under attack from above.

In sum, the changing relationships between senior American career bureaucrats and executive and legislative politicians are set in the context of competition for the wielding of political authority. That competition has been a major factor in promoting the growth and, especially, the importance of both executive and legislative staffs.

While this analysis has emphasized the importance of conflict, it would be misleading to suggest that American government is merely a slightly civilized version of the Hobbesian war of all against all. Most of the time in most of the functioning relationships within departments, political appointees and senior

civil servants coexist reasonably harmoniously and even productively. But when presidential administrations target particular
programs or activities and do so, as they often do, with a heavy
hand, discord ripens and attitudes of distrust become prominent. These situations may be exceptional, but they are the ones
that set the tone for overall politician-bureaucrat relationships.

IMPLICATIONS FOR U.S.–JAPANESE RELATIONS

Despite their common democratic underpinnings, the structure
and spirit of American and Japanese governing processes are
more different than similar. To be sure, each system has large
elements of localism and clientelism, and neither is immune
from particularistic politics. The differences between them,
nevertheless, are large.

The American system is pervaded with conflict. Although
centrism has been developed in the form of the modern presidency, structurally, government in the United States lacks a
center. Even on foreign policy questions, presidential centrism
does not go unchallenged, because Congress is a powerful political actor as well. The political divisions between the President
and Congress in recent decades magnify this constitutionally
mandated conflict.

The American system makes it difficult to unify anything,
the civil service included. Senior career officials increasingly
have had their role in the governing process diminished, while
functional but noncareer (and usually younger) political staffers
have become relatively more important in both the executive and
the legislative branches.

In Japan, too, politicians have become relatively more activ-
ist and powerful *vis-à-vis* the career bureaucracy in recent years.
Still, formal structure aside, Japan has been ruled by a single
party virtually continuously under the postwar Constitution.
The resulting policy continuity and established set of relationships between the LDP and the bureaucracy has no parallel in the
United States.

In both countries, highly talented people come into positions of considerable responsibility. The route taken in Japan is

typically through the career civil service system. In the United States, the pathways are more numerous. As noted, an increasingly important, and distinctive, set of paths are those leading to important staff positions in the White House (and elsewhere in the executive branch) and on Capitol Hill. More and more, knowledge and expertise are packaged in Republican and Democratic forms, a reflection of the intense competition for political power between groups with differing philosophies in the United States. By contrast, the competition for ruling positions within Japan generally has taken the form of factional politics within the LDP.

Although one can say that the process of governing takes place in a rather more continuously serene setting in Japan than in the United States, it is not always obvious just what difference this difference makes. Political stability, of course, suggests policy stability, and, as Taizo Yakushiji points out in his essay on the Japanese system, the political fortunes of the LDP have seemed remarkably immune from adverse conditions, at least until recently. The Japanese perspective, therefore, can be longer term—not necessarily wiser, but longer. Yet, while the more dynamic and conflictual American system stresses short-run political advantage—a necessity in a more uncertain political environment—there also are many examples of stability. Like the LDP in Japan, the Democratic majority in Congress exists in a state of semipermanence, also seemingly immunized against judgments about performance. Its senior staff has continuity and provides a line of defense on behalf of career program bureaucrats in the executive branch. And, as presidents repeatedly learn, the power of the bureaucracy gained both through its expertise and through its responsibility for implementation is substantial and has a leavening effect on efforts to alter policies dramatically.

In many respects, each society's governing processes fit well with other elements of social and economic behavior. The longer-run perspective of the Japanese system gives more emphasis to the development of networks and expectations regarding future behavior than is so in the American case. At the same time, Japan has less need than the United States to accommodate "surges of opinion," and thus shifts in popular attitudes and ideas about public policy are apt to gain greater currency, and to do so more quickly, in the United States.

Each country, then, has ample instances of both stability and change, localism (with particularistic payoffs to clienteles) and attention to broader national interests. On balance, however, governing in the United States follows a less consensual and less stable pattern than is evident in Japan, but one that may (for both better and worse) be more susceptible to—and nourished by— strong popular ideas.

NOTES

1. As President Nixon put it in his memoirs:
   Researchers Joel Aberbach and Bert Rockman found that in 1970 only 17 percent of the top career bureaucrats in the executive branch were Republican; 47 percent were Democrats and 36 percent were independents, who "more frequently resemble Democrats than Republicans." The authors of this study confirm that the frustration we felt with the bureaucracy was based on solid reasons: "Our findings document a career bureaucracy with very little Republican representation but even more pointedly portray a social service bureaucracy dominated by administrators ideologically hostile to many of the directions pursued by the Nixon administration in the realm of social policy." A different study, by Bernard Mennis, concentrated on the foreign service bureaucracy and found that only 5 percent of foreign service officers considered themselves Republicans.
   See, Richard M. Nixon, *RN: The Memoirs of Richard Nixon* (New York: Grosset & Dunlap, 1978), p. 768. For the sources cited, see Joel D. Aberbach and Bert A. Rockman, "Clashing Beliefs Within the Executive Branch: The Nixon Administration Bureaucracy," *American Political Science Review* 70 (June 1976): pp. 456–468; and Bernard Mennis, *American Foreign Policy Officials: Who They Are and What They Believe Regarding International Politics* (Columbus: The Ohio State University Press, 1971), p. 121.
2. For this over-time comparison, see Joel D. Aberbach and Bert A. Rockman, "From Nixon's Problem to Reagan's Achievement," in Larry Berman, ed., *Looking Back On the Reagan Presidency* (Baltimore: The Johns Hopkins University Press, 1990). While in 1970, only 17 percent of the top civil servants were Republicans, by 1986–87 a plurality of 44 percent of a similar group were Republicans. In the meantime, though, while two-thirds of the Nixon appointees in 1970 were Republicans, 94 percent of Reagan's were. Attitudes about policy and party are closely correlated at each point in time.
3. Martin Anderson, *Revolution* (San Diego: Harcourt Brace Jovanovich, 1988), pp. 246–248.

7

POLITICAL CONSTRAINTS IN JAPANESE POLICYMAKING

Taizo Yakushiji

Most people believe that national policies, whether concerning domestic or international affairs, must ultimately be addressed by the state's political head and that he or she will act by exercising the power derived from his or her political base. Hence the assumption that when serious conflicts in policy arise between two nations—such as the current dispute between the United States and Japan over "Super Article 301" of the 1988 U.S. Trade Bill—it will be the respective heads of state who are most responsible for guiding their nations to some sort of conciliation. Thus, in the case of the Trade Bill conflict, the Japanese may be justified in believing that the U.S. designation of Japan as a country engaging in unfair trade practices reflects the policy of the Bush administration, even though technically this designation was made by the U.S. Trade Representative, Carla Hills.

However, Japan's official reaction came not from then Prime Minister Noboru Takeshita, but from Cabinet Secretary Ichiro Obuchi. The Prime Minister only commented in an informal press interview that it was a regrettable incident. This does not mean that Takeshita was too busy in the political turmoil of the Recruit scandal or too ineffective as a lame-duck premier to handle U.S.–Japan trade problems. Instead, it indicates that Japan's prime minister does not voice his comments on highly politicized issues in foreign affairs. This is not merely a technical point of who articulates policies or views, as in the U.S. case; it is a basic political reality that the Prime Minister is primarily oriented toward domestic affairs, and these are not closely linked to international ones. This orientation marks a significant difference between American and Japanese heads of state.

Conventional wisdom about any democratic polity is that voters more or less choose through general elections their state's political head—either a president or a prime minister, depending on the political system. In America, for example, the President is elected by the electoral college, but the electoral college is chosen through direct mass election. In the United Kingdom, Margaret Thatcher has been in office for ten years because her Conservative Party has achieved consecutive victories in national elections over the contending Labour Party.

In Japan, the Prime Minister is chosen not directly by general elections, but through consensus within the ruling Liberal Democratic Party (LDP). This unique selection process is possible because the LDP has stayed in power without interruption since 1955 when two conservative parties, the Liberal Party and the Democratic Party, were unified. In the same year, the left-wing Socialist Party merged with the party of the right-wing socialists (namely, the Social Democrats). Japan's political system since that year has been called the Year-55 Regime.

EX-BUREAUCRATS AND THE YEAR-55 REGIME

In the early period of the Year-55 Regime, the LDP was led by high-ranking ex-bureaucrats, most of whom later became prime ministers or important cabinet ministers. For example, Prime Minister Yoshida had been Ambassador to England; Prime Minister Kishi was from the MCI (the prewar body of the present Ministry of International Trade and Industry, MITI); Prime Minister Ikeda had served as Vice Minister of Finance (Ministry of Finance, MOF); Prime Minister Sato was from the Ministry of Railroads; and Prime Ministers Fukuda and Ohira had both been high-ranking officials at the MOF.

The reason the LDP was led by ex-government officials can be explained by the fact that the postwar economic and social reforms were Japan's most important political targets, and these goals served to guide the government, the primary vehicle in establishing legislative arrangements for postwar recovery. The support by the majority of Japanese of this de facto "coalition" between the LDP and the government—and hence the oppor-

tunity for the experienced ex-bureaucrats to serve in high office—allowed the LDP to rule this country entirely in the Year-55
Regime period.

To combat the conservative regime, the opposition parties
increasingly became ideologically driven. They labeled as status
quo the stance of both the LDP and the government. The issue of
renewal of the U.S.–Japan Security Treaty in 1960 intensified
the ideological identification of the opposition parties. Meanwhile, however, the public became more concerned about individual economic welfare and gradually withdrew partisan
support for the opposition. This, in turn, helped the LDP to stay
in power continuously.

Since the two conservative parties merged in 1955, the LDP
has been a conglomerate of miniparties. And, at least until now,
prime ministers have been chosen by consensus among these
miniparties. However, perhaps as a consequence of the LDP's
long reign, its intraparty struggles to choose prime ministers
have become increasingly contentious and have led to the formation of different factions within the LDP. There are now five
major factions in the party.

"GRAFTED DEMOCRACY" AND PORK-BARREL POLITICS

The intraparty conflict has resulted in severe competition
among the LDP candidates in elections. The Japanese electoral
system is such that constituencies are divided into medium sizes,
a majority of which are allotted an odd number of seats, say three
or five. This aggravates the competition within the party. Take a
three-seat constituency, for example. One seat usually goes to a
prominent politician from a conservative camp who has long had
influence in a local community; the second typically goes to a
coalition candidate of the opposition parties. Then the question
is who will fill the last seat. The last one is often sought competi-
tively by the LDP candidates, who fight each other for party
endorsements.

This intensive electoral battle leads to the candidates' strong
tendency to focus on how much they can address local commu-

nity interests. Campaign issues become more and more locally oriented rather than national in scope, thereby giving birth to pork-barrel politics and alienation from national policy concerns. Thus, foreign policy, for example, is not a good campaign issue on which to win an election in Japan today.

When the ex-bureaucrats held political power in the LDP, the division between their focus on national policies and the concentration on pork-barrel politics by the locally elected officials worked rather nicely. However, this "balance" has been weakened as the pork-barrel politicians have gradually increased their power by ousting the ex-bureaucrats from central positions. This power change was the inevitable consequence of the development of Japanese postwar democracy. Let us focus on this point for a moment.

The General Headquarters of the Allied Forces (GHQ), led by General Douglas MacArthur, tried to democratize Japan. That is, the GHQ meant to impose American democratic principles on Japan's prewar policymaking system. It abolished the powerful prewar government organizations, such as the Ministry of War and the Ministry of Transportation and Telecommunications. Most important, it eliminated the Ministry of Interior, which was the most powerful government agency in prewar Japan and was responsible for appointing prefectural governors as well as local police chiefs. The GHQ proceeded to democratize prefectural politics by introducing gubernatorial elections modeled on the American state system's. However, today, more than 70 percent of the prefectures' annual budgets are subsidized by the central government, so their autonomy is severely limited. Thus, though in many respects the political system of the Japanese prefectures is similar to the American system, a critical difference is that, while prefectural governors are powerful in the local community, they are not so influential in national politics and are not, for example, contenders in prime ministerial races.

So, while the GHQ succeeded in Americanizing Japan's local politics, it failed to Americanize national politics. The democratization of Japan was only half completed; the reason for this was the emergence of the Cold War. With the outbreak of the

Korean War, the GHQ changed its occupation policy to place priority on the postwar recovery of Japan to combat potential communist infiltration. At this point, the GHQ decided to allow prewar high-ranking ex-bureaucrats, previously barred from government, to reenter national politics as central policymakers. Therefore, at the local level an American-style democratic system was in place, while at the national level the prewar policy-making style was preserved. In other words, American-style democracy was only grafted onto the prewar Japanese political system.

This hybrid democratic system facilitated the recruitment of locally based national politicians with pork-barrel political bases. Ex-bureaucrat politicians could exercise their power only as long as Japanese postwar recovery remained the state mission. When economic and social recovery was completed, a change in the balance of power occurred. Since the late 1960s, locally-based politicians have outnumbered ex-bureaucrats in the LDP. The nomination of Kakuei Tanaka as Prime Minister in 1972 marked such a turning point and was the foreseeable consequence of the grafting process.

FROM PARTISAN VOTERS TO ISSUE VOTERS: THE JAPANESE CASE

American voters changed from partisan voting to issue voting around the early 1970s. Up to the late 1960s, Americans cast their presidential votes on the basis of their traditional partisan ideology. Traditionally, southern states, for example, normally supported a Democratic candidate, while midwestern states typically cast votes for a Republican candidate. This partisan voting pattern held until the 1968 election, when Richard Nixon defeated Hubert Humphrey by gaining only 301 electoral votes. His victory was aided by the split of the Democrats between Humphrey and George Wallace, plus the antiwar support for Eugene McCarthy.

The notable shift came in the 1972 election, in which the incumbent Nixon won a landslide victory by gaining an incredible 520 electoral votes. His opponent, George McGovern, got only 17 electoral votes. Before the election Nixon flew to Beijing, and afterward the Paris Accord was put in effect, ending the lingering Vietnam War. Because of this tremendous success in the foreign policy arena, Nixon's postelection popularity reached more than 60 percent.

Given this landslide victory, American political scientists concluded that voters had become more and more issue-oriented. Their rationale was simply that hitherto the presidential candidates had been too similar to each other on the ideological scale, so voters had relied on their traditional partisan stance. However, McGovern's strongly liberal inclinations aroused voters' concerns about campaign issues of domestic as well as international consequence.

The shift from partisan voting to issue voting can also be seen among Japanese voters under the Year-55 Regime. The LDP's popularity began declining in the 1960s and continued to fall into the late 1970s. This trend contradicts the political-economy thesis, which tells us that if economic performance is good, the popularity of an incumbent cabinet will increase. All economic statistics attest to Japan's economic miracle in the 1960s during LDP rule; thus, support should have increased. Why was the reverse true?

One possible explanation is that voters during the period of economic recovery were essentially partisan voters who supported the "coalition" between the government and the LDP. They appreciated government initiatives to lead Japanese economic recovery, and expressed this appreciation by voting for the LDP. However, as recovery came to an end, the role of government officials in legislative activity waned. (Note that a majority of Japanese bills are drafted and introduced by government officials, not by legislative aides, as in the U.S. Congress.) And, as the importance of bureaucrats declined, more of Japan's partisan voters gradually withdrew their support of the LDP.

However, this does not mean that they started to back the opposition parties, since, as mentioned above, the ideological orientation of the latter did not appeal to them, either. Instead, voters became more and more "life-conservative"—that is, concerned with protecting their own economic life. This growing trend was reversed by the oil shocks of 1973 and 1979. Then, the life-conservative voters jumped back onto the bandwagon of LDP support, rationalizing that the LDP was the only party that could be relied upon to solve Japan's economic problems, which were becoming increasingly intermingled with the global economy and, in particular, with the U.S. economy. In other words, they expected that the LDP could handle these problems politically.

This expectation led to the landslide victory of Yasuhiro Nakasone and his cabinet in 1986. Nakasone's performance on the international scene, such as at the seven-nation Economic Summit meetings and in the "Ron-Yasu" friendship with Ronald Reagan, no doubt contributed to his victory. But, according to a survey conducted in the aftermath of the 1986 election, many—perhaps 80 percent—of those who voted for the LDP were no longer loyal partisan sympathizers but simply life-conservatives. One consequence of this fact is that these same voters strongly opposed attempts by both the Nakasone and the Takeshita cabinets to introduce a sales tax, which they regarded as a threat to their economic life. Moreover, with less blind loyalty to the LDP, they are also angry about the Recruit scandal, in which many LDP politicians accepted contributions and profitable insider tips from a private firm seeking influence.

RECRUITMENT OF YOUNG POLITICIANS, NEW BREEDS

The separation between national and local issues, and the loss of political edge for the national issues, was a consequence of grafted democracy. The loss of prestige of government officials and the rising intervention of pork-barrel politics into national policymaking hindered Japan's handling of external economic problems, which are certainly structural in nature.

The structural reform of Japanese politics will have to come about primarily through the reshuffling of politicians. Although the LDP has stayed in power for nearly 35 years, its internal configuration has undergone constant structural changes during this period through the incorporation of politicians of younger generations, the so-called new political breeds. However, as mentioned above, since the intraparty competition to win elections is very intense, it is not easy for new recruits to enter national politics directly. Statistics show that more than 90 percent of the LDP's new recruits come from either those who inherited political positions from retiring senior politicians, sometimes through marriage to their daughters; ex-secretaries of senior politicians; or those who climbed up a local political ladder.

Looked at from the perspective of social background, while the recruitment process of the Japan Socialist Party (JSP) has remained rigid, with a majority of its new recruits (especially in the more powerful lower house) still coming from high posts in labor unions, in contrast, new LDP recruits reflect the LDP's pluralistic characteristics as a "catchall party." They are largely from three groups: ex-bureaucrats (about 10 percent of new recruits); the main faction in power (the Prime Minister's faction); and antibureaucratic locally based politicians. The composition of the second category varies, of course, depending on who is prime minister at the time of the recruits' respective elections. Recently, the second and third groups have intermingled, isolating the first.

Although structural reform of the LDP is moving slowly, the party is becoming more responsive to voters' demands on the local level. On the other hand, on a national level, the Japan Socialist Party has recently become more responsive than the LDP, mainly because the JSP is a national-issue-oriented party backed by the nationally-organized labor unions and teachers' unions, while, in the LDP, the locally-oriented politicians are increasingly more influential than national issue-oriented ex-bureaucrat politicians. Such differences in political inclinations of the two parties resulted in the recent upper house election on July 23, 1989, where the LDP lost its majority (though it is still the single largest party in that chamber).

All survey research data before the elections forecast the LDP's defeat, so that the election result was not much of a surprise to most Japanese. In fact, the victory of the Japan Socialist Party and the defeat of the LDP can be explained by the same logic. First, the sales tax was too unfavorable to most voters who had cast their votes for the LDP three years before. They voted for the Socialist candidates this time, not because they supported them ideologically, but because they wanted to express their anger against the LDP, which had hurried the introduction of the sales tax without hearing much of voters' opinions. Second, the campaign strategy of the JSP to recruit fresh candidates (even though, as noted, a majority are still labor union leaders) worked well to attract life-conservative and angry voters. Third, a careful approach to the introduction of the new sales tax could not have been taken within the LDP since the tax issue is a national issue and a majority of the LDP's politicians are more concerned with local issues to win interfactional fights in elections for the more important lower house.

WILL THE YEAR-55 REGIME END?

In American politics, despite his 1972 landslide victory, Richard Nixon suffered a sharp decline in popularity a year later because of the Watergate scandal. In Japanese politics, Nakasone, who once gained a landslide victory, lost local elections in the Iwate and Fukuoka Prefectures in 1987; as reported worldwide, he suffered further from the Recruit scandal. Prime Minister Takeshita, who was Nakasone's personal choice, suffered a sharp decline in popularity toward the end of his term in 1989, and, like Nixon, resigned.

It appears mysterious that such sharp declines in popularity happen within relatively short periods. But it is not all mystery, and some explanation should be possible. One explanation may be based on both the shift of voters from partisan orientation to issue orientation and the inability of "supply-side politics" to deal with that shift.

First of all, the landslide victories of both Nixon and Nakasone were attributable to issue voters—Americans who appreciated Nixon's economic and diplomatic actions, and Japanese who valued Nakasone's diplomatic successes. These voters were no longer the partisan supporters who gave Nixon and Nakasone marginal victories in 1968 and 1983, respectively. Still, as issue-concerned voters, they easily turned against the incumbent when they thought that new policies would infringe on their lives. Nixon's "Saturday Night Massacre," in which he dismissed the Watergate Special Prosecutor, and his blunt request that Americans turn down the temperature of their homes by six degrees, triggered an adverse reaction. Nakasone's introduction of a sales tax ignited a similar reaction. Both leaders mistakenly thought they possessed mandates to implement new policies because of their previous overwhelming victories.

Moreover, neither administration was aware of the shift of voters, each erroneously believing that partisan loyalists had caused his landslide win. As a result, they delayed the necessary reshuffling of the political structure and, instead, tried to deal with the change in "demand-side politics" through diplomatic maneuvers. Nixon's diplomatic intervention into the October 1973 Middle East War and Nakasone's inviting President Reagan to his villa exemplify this.

Despite all the differences between their political systems, Japanese voters are becoming more like their American counterparts. Synchronization of the economies of the two countries and the narrowing gaps of per capita incomes are perhaps the key economic explanations for the resemblance between Japanese and U.S. voting behavior. However, there still remains a structural difference in political systems of the two countries.

In the United States, democratic politics operate on two levels, the presidential level and the state and local level. However, Americans did not introduce the presidential system into Japan, whereas they introduced it in Korea. Instead, the GHQ put more emphasis on national political stability and preferred a conservative government. But it emancipated local politics, and from this arena came the politicians who have infiltrated the conservative party. The high political stability Japan has long maintained has been possible only at the expense of the weakening of the state political head, the Prime Minister. In other words, Japan's political stability stemmed from a wide coverage of political constituencies by the ruling party. Such a wide coverage of political markets is a consequence of intraparty competition among different LDP factions that try to exploit new voters' support. Intraparty competition and confrontation are so intense in the LDP that, in order to avoid splitting the party, rules needed to be established to select the head of the party. The result is a process in which the party president, who is (or at least up to now, has been) automatically the Prime Minister of Japan, is selected as a consensus choice. The fact that he has been chosen not because his party won the election on the basis of its stand on certain key national issues, but, rather, because political compromises have been made among other competing faction leaders within the ruling LDP, creates a dilemma for Japan's Prime Minister if he seeks to exercise real power or pursue controversial policies.

Japanese voters are frustrated not only with the Recruit scandal per se, but, more important, with the structural defects of their country's peculiar political system that has been in place for 35 years. The grafted democracy that is the dominant political factor of the Year-55 Regime is, as we have noted, a hybrid of the prewar political style on a national level and the new American-flavored liberalized politics on the local level. As time has gone on, grafted democracy has helped pork-barrel politicians to be recruited to national politics. They have gradually come to outnumber the prewar-style political elites who were more concerned with national or international issues. The consequence is obvious: there has emerged a vacuum of political leverage—and vision—to steer national and international issues. To those who came from strong pork-barrel constituencies, backing a national or international issue is not an attractive way to help increase political support. It is then ironic to say that, while the grafted democracy which resulted from an incomplete implantation of American democracy in fact created Japanese political stability, it also stripped power from the center of politics, namely from government and from national and international policy-conscious politicians. The Recruit scandal could yet mark a farewell to the Year-55 Regime. If so, then the question becomes: What kind of political system will come next?

APPENDIX

*Conference on Social Change in
Japan and the United States:
Implications for the Bilateral Relationship*

*December 10–11, 1988
Oiso, Japan*

JAPANESE PARTICIPANTS

Satsuki Eda, *United Social Democratic Party*
Masumi Ishikawa, *The Asahi Shimbun*
Shojiro Imanishi, *National Institute for Research Advancement*
Sumiko Iwao, *Keio University*
Soshichi Miyachi, *The Nihon Keizai Shimbun*
Takuya Negami, *Kobe Steel Ltd.*
Yoshiji Nogami, *Japan Institute of International Affairs*
Sadako Ogata, *National Institute for Research Advancement and
    Sophia University*
Haruo Shimada, *Keio University*
Atsushi Shimokobe, *National Institute for Research Advancement*
Tasuku Takagaki, *The Bank of Tokyo, Ltd.*
Taizo Yakushiji, *Saitama University*
Tadashi Yamamoto, *Japan Center for International Exchange*

U.S. PARTICIPANTS

James C. Abegglen, *Asia Advisory Service and Sophia University*
Susan Chira, *The New York Times*
Rust M. Deming, *American Embassy, Tokyo*
Jeffrey E. Garten, *Eliot Group, Inc.*
Louis Gerber, *Communications Workers of America, AFL-CIO*
William H. Gleysteen, Jr., *Council on Foreign Relations*

Neil Goldschmidt, *State of Oregon*
Steven Hofman, *Republican Research Committee, House of Representatives*
Scott Lilly, *Democratic Study Group, House of Representatives*
Bert A. Rockman, *University of Pittsburgh*
Alan D. Romberg, *Council on Foreign Relations*
Howard Schuman, *University of Michigan*
Peter Tarnoff, *Council on Foreign Relations*
D. Eleanor Westney, *Massachusetts Institute of Technology*
Daniel Yankelovich, *The Daniel Yankelovich Group, Inc.*

INDEX

ABOUT THE AUTHORS AND EDITORS

Sumiko Iwao is Professor of Social Psychology at the Institute of Communications Research of Keio University. Prior to joining the Institute, Professor Iwao was on the faculty of Harvard University, the University of Tokyo, and Tsukuba University. Among her recent publications are *The Images of Japan in the Eyes of Foreign Students* (1987) and *Foreign Students in Japan* (1988).

Bert A. Rockman is Professor of Political Science and Research Professor at the University Center for International Studies at the University of Pittsburgh. He is also Senior Fellow, Government Studies Program, at the Brookings Institution. His publications include *Bureaucrats and Politicians in Western Democracies,* co-authored with Joel D. Aberbach and Robert D. Putnam (1981), and "Comparing Japanese and American Bureaucrats," *British Journal of Political Science,* co-authored with Joel D. Aberbach, Ellis S. Krauss, and Michio Muramatsu (1990).

Alan D. Romberg is the C.V. Starr Fellow for Asia at the Council on Foreign Relations. During his 20-year career in the Foreign Service he specialized in East Asian affairs and was Director of the Office of Japanese Affairs from 1978 to 1980. Among his publications are *U.S.–Japan Relations: A Partnership in Search of Definition* (Critical Issues 1988:1) and *The United States, the Soviet Union, and Korea: Beyond Confrontation* (Critical Issues 1989:1).

Howard Schuman is Professor, Department of Sociology, at the University of Michigan, Director of the Survey Research Center at the Institute for Social Research, and Editor of *Public Opinion Quarterly.* Among his articles and books are *Questions and Answers in Attitude Surveys: Experiments in Question, Form, Wording and Context,* with Stanley Presser (1981), and *Racial Attitudes in Amer-*

137

ica: Trends and Interpretations, with Charlotte Steeh and Lawrence Bobo (1985).

Haruo Shimada is Professor of Economics at Keio University and Visiting Researcher at the Japan Institute of Labor. He was Visiting Principal Research Officer at the Economic Research Institute of the Economic Planning Agency, as well as Visiting Professor at both the Massachusetts Institute of Technology's Sloan School of Management and the E.S.S.E.C. in Paris. He is the author of *The Frontier of Labor Economics* (1977) and *The Economics of Humanware* (1988).

D. Eleanor Westney is Associate Professor of Management at the Massachusetts Institute of Technology's Sloan School of Management and is currently (1989–1990) Toyota Visiting Professor at the University of Michigan Center for Japanese Studies. Her publications include *Imitation and Innovation: The Transfer of Western Organizational Patterns to Meiji Japan* (1987) and "Sociological Approaches to the Pacific Region," *The Annals of the American Academy of Political and Social Science* (September 1989).

Taizo Yakushiji is Professor of Technology and International Relations at the Graduate Institute of Political Science at Saitama University. He was a Fulbright Scholar and a Ford Foundation Fellow. His recent publications include *Public Policy* (1989) and *Techno-hegemony* (1989).

Tadashi Yamamoto is President and Chairman of the Board of the Japan Center for International Exchange (JCIE), which he founded in 1970. Mr. Yamamoto is engaged in promoting international communication, stimulating research on international issues involving Japan, and encouraging international exchange by private Japanese organizations. He is currently a member and the Japanese Director of the Trilateral Commission, a member of the U.K.–Japan 2000 Group and of the Korea-Japan 21st Century Committee, and was a member of the Prime Minister's Private Council on International Cultural Exchange established in May 1988.

*The Council on Foreign Relations publishes authoritative and
timely books on international affairs and American foreign policy. Designed for the interested citizen and specialist alike, the
Council's rich assortment of studies covers topics ranging from
economics to regional conflict to East-West relations. If you would
like more information, please write:*

Council on Foreign Relations Press
58 East 68th Street
New York, NY 10021
Telephone: (212) 734-0400
FAX: (212) 861-1789